MAKING MONEY MAKING MOVIES

SHELDON TROMBERG

MAKING MONEY MAKING MOVIES

THE INDEPENDENT MOVIE-MAKERS' HANDBOOK

NEW VIEWPOINTS/VISION BOOKS
A DIVISION OF FRANKLIN WATTS
NEW YORK/LONDON

NEW VIEWPOINTS/VISION BOOKS
A DIVISION OF FRANKLIN WATTS
730 FIFTH AVENUE
NEW YORK, NEW YORK 10019

Library of Congress Cataloging in Publication Data

Tromberg, Sheldon.
    Making money, making movies.

    Includes index.
    1. Moving-picture authorship. 2. Moving-
pictures—Production and direction. 3. Moving-
pictures—Distribution. 4. Moving-picture   industry. I. Title.
PN1996.T7   791.43   79-18245
ISBN 0-531-06370-4
ISBN 0-531-06753-X pbk.

CONTENTS

	Foreword	1
	Preface	3
	Introduction	5
	PART 1. SCREENWRITING	**7**
Chapter 1.	**Screenwriting: Say What You Mean**	**9**
	Self-Discipline	10
	On The One Hand- On The Other Hand: An Essential Screenwriting Device	12
	Take A Break	14
	Inner Ear, Inner Eye	14
	Subject, Verb, Object	16

Chapter 2. Define, Describe, Compare, Contrast 18

Wizards of Phantasm 23

Nuances and Hooks 26

Let's Suppose 29

Chapter 3. The Good Guy and the Bad Guy 33

Conflict 34

Dialogue Cutaway 36

Creative Use of Available Resources 37

Write Your Review 38

Chapter 4. Writing to Order 42

Step By Step 45

Screenwriting Tips 47

Wake-Up Exercises 51

PART 2. PRODUCTION 53

Chapter 5. Movies and the Aspiring Independent 55

Your $750,000 Movie 57

Budgeting Your $750,000 Movie 58

Chapter 6. Below-the-Line Costs 64

Production Staff 64

Balance of Your Production Staff 70

Post Production 82

Studios and On-Site Locations 85

Chapter 7. Caution: Don't Promise to Make a Movie 90

The Proposal: Full Disclosure 91

Chapter 8. The Process of Production   **98**

    Preproduction   98

    The Script   105

    Shot List   118

    Making It   122

PART 3. DISTRIBUTION   **127**

Chapter 9. Distribution: The Middleman   **129**

    Key Cities   131

    Three Types of Distribution Deals   138

Chapter 10. Distributors and Exhibitors:
An Ongoing Relationship   **146**

    Be Your Own Distributor   148

    Exhibition Contract   153

    Film Rental Terms   154

PART 4. EXHIBITION   **159**

Chapter 11. Retailing Movies   **161**

    Exhibition and the Independent
    Producer–Distributor   164

    House Nuts   167

Chapter 12. Releasing a Movie to Exhibitors   **170**

PART 5. SHORT TAKES   **177**

    Glossary   195
    Index   201

ACKNOWLEDGMENTS

Thanks to the true-blue people whose
encouragement helped me reach this goal:

Gary Arnold, Isaac Bein, John G. Broumas, Charles
Conconi, E. Charles Costolo, Otto Ebert, Mary
Murtagh, Rox Palese, James Lister Potts, Paul Roth,
Elias Savada, Joy and Norman Silverman, George
Somma, Peter Thomas, Stephen Michael Trattner,
John Treanor, Harry Tromberg, James R. Velde, and
Les Whitten.

I DEDICATE THIS BOOK TO JESSIE,
BRUCE, MELISSA, AND ALICIA

Making money is art and
good business is the best art.
                —ANDY WARHOL

I believe in the exceptional man—
the entrepreneur who is always
running out of money, not the
bureaucrat who generates
cash flow and pays dividends.
                —ARMAND ERPF

In order to be a great writer
a person must have a built-in,
shockproof crap detector.
                —ERNEST HEMINGWAY

Statistics are no substitute for judgment.
                —HENRY CLAY

Between the idea and the reality,
between the motion and the act,
falls the shadow.
                —T.S. ELIOT

It is only with the heart one
can see rightly; what is essential
is invisible to the eye.
                —FROM THE LITTLE PRINCE

"Let's go to the movies."
"Let's take the children to the movies."
"The children went to the movies with their friends."
"Let's go to the movies with the children."
"The children went to the movies with their dates."
"Let's go to the movies."
                —MY WIFE, JESSIE

MAKING
MONEY
MAKING
MOVIES

FOREWORD

Sheldon Tromberg is unique. He has a span of credentials that are matched by few, if any, in the eighty-year history of the motion-picture industry. I know. I've been in the movie business for fifty-one years. For twenty-five of those years I've observed Tromberg's career. He's gone from industry trainee with Republic Pictures to a mature renaissance movie man, excelling in a variety of positions. He's an experienced screenwriter, producer, distributor, exhibitor, educator, and drama critic for Washington, D.C.'s ABC-TV affiliate, a major newspaper columnist, and an NBC-radio-affiliate talk-show host.

Sheldon established milestone motion-picture courses, first at Georgetown University, then at the Corcoran School of Art. Many of his former students have successfully entered the industry, serving in a variety of posts with major motion-picture companies. They like to call themselves "Tromberg's Troupers."

I've seen Sheldon in action—on location, in the office, boardroom, and in the classroom. He communicates knowledge, inspires understanding, and motivates beginners and experienced professionals alike to achieve greater heights of excellence.

Many of us in the industry encouraged Sheldon to write this book. It is the first essential industry work, destined to become a landmark guide for anyone interested in a comprehensive understanding of the movie world.

It is with pride that I recommend this indispensable book to you, the movie public.

JOHN G. BROUMAS, PRESIDENT
SHOWCASE THEATRES
WASHINGTON, D.C.
1979

PREFACE

So you want to make movies? Try telling that to your parents and they'll likely ask you why you don't get a *regular* job. They have a point to make. They want to know whether you consider moviemaking a hobby or profession. They'll want to see some evidence that you have a solid background in your field of study, a seriousness of purpose, a personal commitment to succeed, a willingness to learn, and *a chance to earn a living*. None of it is easy. Some of it is downright difficult. One thing I've observed over the years: The ones who do succeed are voracious readers and go about their work as if pursued by a devil. Right from the start, you'll want to make every effort to gain a body of knowledge about the motion-picture industry. If you ever have the chance to join the crew of a major movie production on location, grab it. Grab it no matter how menial the job. If you can create the opportunity, so much the better. A physician interns in a hospital, a ball player practices on a field of play, yet so many who want to be part of the moviemaking process have no location to go to for practice.

Although there is no substitute for movie studio and location work, there are many aspects of the whole process—

from production through distribution through exhibition—that can and must be learned; I have tried to address myself to all of these areas. My efforts are directed to those among you who want or need some alternative to actual studio-office and/or location work, or, perhaps, to supplement your college film courses. In any event, it's the first-timer or even the second- or third-timer who may not have accomplished everything on the first try that this book is written for. Moreover, for anyone interested in just how this industry works, I hope this book provides at least an introduction to that elusive something, that will-o'-the-wisp, that industry old-timers called "the picture business."

Whatever. Movies are made for money.

Or glory.

But, mostly for money.

INTRODUCTION

There are three basic pillars to the single-purpose structure commonly called the motion-picture industry: production, distribution, and exhibition.

Production deals with the creation of the product we call a motion picture. Distribution, the center pillar, is concerned with getting the motion picture into the marketplace. Exhibition is the marketplace, where commercial theaters exhibit the motion picture for an admission price.

Some pundits refer to production as manufacturing, to distributors as wholesalers, and to exhibitors as retailers. However we define the industry, it remains a commercial enterprise. But, an uneasy one, because it deals with a commercial art form. A movie is not intended as a free diversion to beguile nonpaying critics in imperishable art museums but as a merchandisable product available to commercial storefront theaters. A movie is a perishable commodity in a theater. It has to do business to enjoy even a brief booking on the cinema screen. To encourage and enhance that possibility, the most commercially appealing and salable features of the movie are advertised. Therefore, the perception that PR personnel accentuate is the metamorphosing of the movie into a slice of entertainment so appetizing and desirable as to make it irresistible to the broadest segments of society—for a price.

You, as an independent moviemaker, must be cognizant of the fact that in the business of movies, art is not independent of commerce. It is a kind of uneasy alliance whereby disparate interests are bonded together by a single goal: getting the best possible movie made and seen by the most people. Part 1 examines the screenwriting process. It all starts with an idea. The idea is developed into a story. Then the story is written in a special form—a script. Most schools teach prose, not scripting. The script form, foreign to so many, is a special part of the production process. To allow for its specialness, I have initially divorced it from the section titled Part 2 Production, but later also integrated it into that section so that, step by step, you can trace the development of the script into a kind of detailed master plan from which you will make your movie.

Once made, your film will have to be distributed, which is discussed in Part 3. The purpose of distribution is to see that the movie is seen, and Part 4, therefore, deals with exhibition, the retailing of movies. Part 5 is a series of personal reflections based on my firsthand experiences in the movie industry.

I hope that the picture is clear—that a movie is a dream come true. My goal is to help you help yourself make it come true.

PART 1

SCREEN· WRITING

CHAPTER 1

SCREENWRITING: SAY WHAT YOU MEAN

Screenwriting isn't a traditional academic subject in American grammar schools. When students of film first enter the world of screenwriting they face a form of expression as strange, brief and to-the-point as a pharmacist's prescription. They become aware for the first time that studying screenplay writing may be as difficult as studying and mastering a foreign language so that it may be spoken and written freely. Screenplay language is, so to speak, the Latin for the whole romance of the movie industry. When studying a foreign language, you must try to *think* in that language, not in English. One of the best ways of going about learning how to think, talk, and write script is to speak it, conversationally, with your fellow students who are also aspiring scripters. Instead of communicating in traditional prose form— word, sentence, paragraph—you'll be mentally numbering your thoughts and stating them in shots, scenes, and sequences so that you make pictures in people's heads. Instead of using commas, semicolons, colons, and dashes, you'll pause and connect your shots, scenes, and sequences with cuts, fades, dissolves, and wipes. It's all part of the special and unique coherency called screenplay talk, a language full of highly visual action images. A step-by-step analysis of a screenplay is discussed in Chapter 8. For now, to take first things first, let's understand some of the concepts.

To be an effective writer you must say exactly what you mean, especially if your specialty is scripting. You must advance your thoughts *visually*, with clarity and dispatch. Movie talk is not real-life talk. It is just movie talk, meant to communicate, along with unspoken dialogue. Everything in a movie is dialogue. *Spoken dialogue accounts for only about 15 to 30 percent of a modern script in terms of eventual screentime.* Other "dialogue" includes sounds, music, special effects, facial expressions, body language, hairstyles, colors, shapes, clothing, makeup, weather, camera movement, and silence.

SELF-DISCIPLINE

Self-discipline will bring your movie idea into sharper focus.

Introductory Premise:
The First Expansion of Your Idea

Most people begin with an idea or notion about what they want to write about. That's a start, but that's all it is. Now, for the first time, you must develop that *beginning* idea into a story with a plausible *middle* and a reasonable *ending*. But the ending isn't the end; the denouement, or *resolution*, is. For example, suppose your story deals with a young man who has a talent for riding motorcycles. His ambition is to be the world's champion rider. Well, along the way he meets obstacles and crises, but by the end of the movie he does become the world champion. However, he remains unsatisfied and resolves to design and build the world's best and safest motorcycle. So he invests his prize money in research and equipment.

Beginning: Ambition to be world's best motorcyclist
Middle: Obstacles and crises along the way
Ending: Wins world's championship;
              ambition fulfilled

Resolution: Invests prize money in research
and equipment
Resolving to build world's
best and safest cycle

Expand your story idea into about eight sentences totaling about 120 words. It's a great exercise in discipline and will force you to become cogent and brief. A good way to begin is with a "Suppose": Suppose something happens, something else happens, conflict arises, there are tensions, confrontations, twists and turns, all the time advancing the story and developing the characters in a way that communicates with worldwide audiences. Finally the ending; does it answer the "Suppose"?

In the finale, the denouement, the main character exits to embark on another adventure, or the character has been developed so that greater goals are set, a new life begun with a clearer understanding of the world.

As an exercise, write down the *theme* of your story. Make it short and pithy. For example, an acceptable theme for the movie *The Turning Point* would be, "you can't have it both ways."

The Premise:
An Expansion of Your
Introductory Premise
To help you help yourself develop your story, put your premise on paper. Without using any spoken dialogue, expand your story, using traditional prose form, into two pages or about 300 to 400 words. Then ask yourself if your story has enough substance to grasp and hold an audience's attention over a ninety-minute period. You've got to develop an "inner ear" to do this—it requires a constant tuning of your own sense and sensibilities about what "works" and what doesn't. How do you tune in to yourself? It isn't easy. It's a kind of process that is enriched and nourished by experience and knowledge, and, especially, by making a picture in your head of exactly what you want to say. The 300- or 400-word premise is a helpful device in the ongoing process of getting in tune with your inner ear and inner eye, of making an in-focus picture of what you "see" in your mind and communicating that precise image to the reader of your script.

Introductory Treatment:
Developing the Premise

It's important to get to *know* your characters. You are creating people, and you'll be "living" with them all the time you're writing your script. Write a biography of each of your lead characters. Write, in random order, where they were born, their family history, friendships, dining preferences, schooling, habits, work and life experiences. You are aiming to define their *personalities,* each one a different and unique human being. Giving one character blond hair and another black hair isn't enough. Nor is making one tall and another short good enough. Beginnings, yes, but too vague in definition. Each one should have a separate set of characteristics. You are beginning to personalize your characters, to bring them to life. You must tackle these efforts with a kind of splendid articulation, with visual clarity.

You have gone a long way toward doing your job if you can now predict with exactitude just how your characters will respond differently to a common situation.

You may have eight schoolteachers about to take a summer vacation. Each of them should have singular preferences for a vacation; each one should prefer a different season, a different part of the world, for varying lengths of time, alone or with diverse people. One might charge the cost of the trip, another pay cash, another win a free trip, another be someone's guest, still another might be a stowaway, yet another might spend the vacation at a second home or with a relative or friend, or be a volunteer for a charity event, or just stay at home. Your objective is clear: Your writing must be explicit, economical, and quintessentially direct.

ON THE ONE HAND—
ON THE OTHER HAND:
AN ESSENTIAL
SCRIPTWRITING DEVICE

On the one hand—on the other hand simply means that every time you give a characteristic to a person or situation you must give an opposite one. For example, if one person drives a new

Cadillac, the other person should drive an old Volkswagen. If one person exits a city bus, the next should debark from a chartered plane. If one person wears spiffy suits, the other should wear rumpled casual clothes. If one prefers rare meat, the other should like only cooked fish. If one is short and squat, the other is tall and lean, remembering that you must define shortness and squatness and tallness and leanness precisely, explicitly, to bring your characters' personalities to the point where you can *see them* when they, so to speak, walk into your living room. They must be vividly alive, and you must make your opposite characters interact, to create drama.

Write about seventy-five words of description for each of your supporting characters. Again, you are aiming to *paint a word picture* of each one. Just as you did for each of your leads, craft a separate set of personality characteristics for each one. Give them the breath of life. Strive for leanness, clarity, style, and irony, all the while detailing your characters.

For example, Joe Winner's got a forest of curly, black hair, a craggy forehead, seashell ears, a dimpled nose, a third-baseman chin, and you can't see his mouth—it's ambushed by a woolly salt-and-pepper moustache. When he speaks, his eyebrows bounce like tennis balls, his mop of hair looks like a sea of asterisks, the lines on his forehead seem to form quotation marks around his phrases, and his upper lip shimmies like a rabbit on a scent.

Now that you have your characters, develop them and reveal them as they are through interrelationships. Expand your premise to about ten to twelve pages, about 2,000 to 3,000 words. For the first time, use illustrative spoken dialogue. Don't use spoken dialogue to create action. Instead, use it only when there is a need to develop the character or advance the story, which cannot, absolutely cannot, be done any other way.

For example, if one of your characters is a "nice person," don't have someone say he's a nice person; reveal it through action. Have Mr. Nice Person help another person in distress, such as aiding a driver push his or her car off a snowy mound or buying a drink for someone who is down and out. You'll be writing shots and scenes that reveal character through action, not words. It helps make your motion picture *move*.

TAKE A BREAK

When you have accomplished this, take a break. Put everything you've written up to this point in a file or envelope and stash it in a drawer. Don't look at it for at least three or four days, no matter how severe the temptation to continue persists. Let your subjectivity, your personal feelings, cool off for a brief period of time. Then, after time has passed, remove the file and review your work. You must not only create, you must learn to be objective enough to blue-pencil, to edit your work, revise it, change it, improve it, solidify your story, theme, and people. At this point you should be objective enough to tackle that task like a hard-nosed editor, seeking clarity, style, irony, wit, content, flow, and rhythm. Is your story reasonable? Is it entertaining? Do your characters react to each other directly? Have you expanded your original idea into a *visual story*? *"Act out" the words and gestures of the different characters.* Does it "play"?

INNER EAR, INNER EYE

You'll be listening to your inner ear, tuning in on your inner eye for filmic expression. You're tuning in on yourself—screen-writing means giving of yourself, wrenching feelings, perceptions, instincts, and reason into words that convey emotions, sounds, and colors in an entertaining, enthralling way.

Use a tape recorder. Play it back. Listen. Does it sound like what you intended it to be? You'll likely want to make changes. Be flexible. Go back to the beginning and refine your thoughts. Nothing of what you write in the process of putting together a screenplay is carved in stone. Like one of the mail-order catalogs advertises, move your script up the line from good to better to the top-of-the-line, best. Best is almost never attainable in scripts, but nearly best is nearly a miracle of achievement. Don't ask your relatives or friends what they think of your work! They won't understand it; they haven't had experience in script writing and, besides, they love you or at least like you. They'll pat you on the head and say everything you've done is great. This is your first introduction to the solitude of writing. You will have to live with it. You will also have to face the hard truth that writing makes you feel very vulnerable. Many writers are sensitive to criticism, some are very sensitive to criticism of any kind, from anyone. Aspiring screenwriters cannot face the present and future without uncertainty about their work. It goes with the craft. Accept it. *Just satisfy yourself, not the whole world.* Are you satisfied with your work so far? If so, proceed to the next assignment.

The Treatment: The Complete
Expression of Your Idea in Prose Form

A treatment is usually between thirty and seventy-five pages. Although this sort of variance may suggest vagueness, nearly all treatments fall into those extremes. Each page of treatment should convert to between two and four minutes of screentime. Essentially a script in prose form, a treatment is the final stage of preparation, just before you tackle the professional script form.

HANDY-DANDY QUESTIONS:
NINE CHARACTERS OR THINGS

Here are some handy-dandy questions for you to ask yourself: Have you created the following nine characters or things?

1. Good (The Good Person)
2. Good's Helpmate
3. Good's Instrument
4. Evil (may also be the Bad Person)
5. Evil's Helpmate
6. Evil's Instrument
7. Everyman (The Ordinary Person)
8. Everyman's Helpmate
9. Everyman's Instrument

The Lone Ranger was Good. Tonto was his Helpmate. He had two Instruments: his horse, Silver, and his silver bullets. Try to find the above nine items in a movie, any movie. They're there, at least one for each of the nine. The better the movie, the more items for each category. Study *Star Wars* and discover several levels of responses for each item.

THREE BASICS

Have you dealt with the three basics—Love, Hate, Death—that are in nearly every movie? Have you introduced them, then interrelated them? Have you used these themes to heighten drama?

SUBJECT, VERB, OBJECT

Have you remembered what your grammar-school teacher told you about an English sentence? Let me remind you once again: The formal construction is subject, verb, object.

Joe walks to the door.
- Who is Joe?
- Why is he walking to the door?
- How does he walk to the door?
  Does he amble, jog, slide, slip, scoot?
- Something should happen as he walks to the door.
  What happens in your story?
- What kind of a door is it? Why?
- What's going to happen when he gets to the door?

Now, suppose the door walks to Joe? Well now, maybe you're writing a horror story. Or suppose the door walks to the door? Well, maybe it's science-fiction. Or, try Joe walks to Joe. Well, maybe he's cloned or stoned or dreaming, or you're on your way to writing a juicy mystery. The thing to remember is that subject-verb-object keeps your story *moving*. It helps to discourage our natural inclinations to write about people staring, walking, talking endlessly, without rhyme or reason. After all, don't you want the audience to wonder what happens next? Certainly you do! When the audience wonders about what's going to happen next, you've got them interested. If you were blowing spitballs through straws or pressing gum on inkwells when grammar was introduced, here's your chance to redeem yourself and benefit, too.

The Script
Think about your story once again. This is your final practice shot before tackling the real thing. Divide your script into fifteen parts, or sequences—perhaps six to eight minutes each—each

one a clearly identifiable period of time. Write down fifteen sentences covering the fifteen sequences. List them. Each sentence should be from five to fifteen words, the shorter the better. Each sequence is to have a point, a specific point that you want to make.

For example, your script might have two characters, Theresa and Joe. One sequence might make the following point: Theresa and Joe meet, fall in love, decide to spend the rest of their lives together, and make plans for their wedding.

These specific points, each with a beginning, middle, and ending, are the items you should list. When you get through listing the fifteen points, you should have 90 to 120 minutes of eventual screentime. It's your story skeleton. Bone up on this technique. It works. It puts things in focus. To be successful, it must flow, so that point 15 answers point 1. Most major movies have thirteen to eighteen sequences: that's it, folks! That's all there is to it, just an average of fifteen short sentences describing fifteen sequences, but each must be coherent and include a beginning, middle, end, and resolution. It isn't too hard, if you think about it. Try it. Try it again. Now, read your sequences aloud. Are you satisfied that each sequence has been pared down to the barest essentials and that this sparse column outline is just what you want to script? Have you left anything out? *Try this on for size:* Each sequence will have about four scenes and each scene will average about four shots. *So, 15 sequences equal 60 scenes equal 240 shots, equals a movie.* We, all of us, must keep *intellectualizing down* to whittle a hand-carved script that has a distinct personality. For example, your first inclination might be that a character in your script will respond to another's question by saying, "Yes, I certainly agree with your thinking, so go ahead with it." But when you write a professional script, you may very well intellectualize down to complete *simplicity* by having your character say nothing. Instead, next to his name you'll describe a one-word action (nods). Are you nodding?

Each page of your script should be about 135 words. That's about forty to sixty seconds of eventual screentime, depending on factors beyond your control: actors, directors, producers, editors, mixers, distributors, censors, and advertisers. They develop the film's rhythm based on your script, and they do make changes! To them you're a writer, not an author!

CHAPTER 2

DEFINE, DESCRIBE, COMPARE, CONTRAST

A script for a ninety-minute film will average between 90 and 120 pages, or between 12,500 and 13,770 words. To put it into perspective, about one-fourth the length of a typical novel. Consequently, with so few words to deal with, you learn quickly that the trick is to reveal things without saying them—to create *action through reaction*. My own formula to begin this process consists of four simple words: define, describe, compare, contrast. That's it! A way of thinking. Four words to glory! Let's take, for example, Theresa:

Define: Female, age 25, healthy
Describe: Here you give her a *personality*
Compare: Here you'll have Theresa mix
Contrast: and mingle with
            other people, all the while
            comparing and contrasting
            her personality with the
            rest of your characters

Theresa may be shy and introverted. When she interacts with gregarious types, extroverts, her character will be revealed by her *reactions* to their actions.

In fashioning a character, first define the character. Then describe that character, visually—make pictures with words! Then, create another character, probably an opposite of character one. Then, again visually, contrast them. Have them clash, conflict, bang heads, move in separate directions, give them different life-styles and let us see pictures of how they react differently to common situations, how one influences the other. For example, if Good meets Evil does Good influence Evil into becoming Good? Or, does Evil influence Good to the point where Good turns to Evil? These situations are found in many westerns, space flicks, horror movies, and just plain mysteries, and even love stories.

For example, it's 1890 and Miss Theresa Elza, a scholarship student, graduates from an eastern nursing school and travels west to Dingwater to join her brother and sister-in-law, dirt-poor farmers. Theresa's Good, 21, innocent, and trying to decide where to practice nursing. In Dingwater, she buckboards to town to pick up some supplies. While there, a shootout occurs and she saves a gunfighter's life. G. C. Barker is on the scene. He's the richest, meanest man in town. He's Bad! He observes Theresa's grace and professional skills. Sure enough, as the story develops, he falls head over heels in love with diminutive Theresa. They marry. He stops gambling and whorin' and builds a town meeting hall and a church. But Theresa develops a knack for business and takes over all his enterprises. She becomes Bad, Barker becomes Good. He's deeply in love with her, but she's more in love with her first taste of power and money than with him. One day a gigolo comes to town and Theresa runs off with him. But time passes and she returns, asking and getting Barker's forgiveness while he's dedicating the town's first hospital.

Theresa: Good, then Evil, then Good
Barker: Evil, then Good

Then, each is a Helpmate,
the Instrument being Love.

SCREENWRITING RACES:
ADJECTIVE 500 AND ADVERB 300

If one of your characters is beautiful, your job as a scriptwriter is to describe your character in such a way that the script reader will *deduce* that the character is beautiful as a result of the word picture you've drawn. Under no circumstances should you say the character is beautiful. Your job is to define and describe her beauty and, if necessary, use adverbs and adjectives to do the job. Racing-car drivers have their races, such as the Indianapolis 500 and Atlanta 300—your races are the Adjective 500 and Adverb 300. They help give final truths to people and places and get your script across the finish line.

For example, is your character *running* or running confidently, running swiftly, dashing violently, or darting quickly? Or does your character run wild, run amuck, sidestep gingerly, saunter and shuffle nonchalantly, stride fully, or strut and swagger easily?

Is your character smiling, just smiling? Smiling hopefully or smiling expectantly or smiling falsely, hard, broadly, warmly, or smiling coldly? Define and describe! That smile will be up on a 720-square-foot screen, not 19 diagonal inches. That smile is projected in theaters as being bigger than life, maybe a few feet tall and a couple of feet wide. It is dialogue, it communicates. What feeling, what emotion do you want it to communicate? Think about it carefully, then write about it, carefully.

Some people try to characterize screenwriters. They call them patternmakers or architects or mapmakers. But screenwriting is screenwriting is screenwriting. It generally means four things in various orders of importance to different moviemakers: story, story, story, and characters; or characters and story, story story; or any combination of story and characters. Lots of people in real estate say that every developer of property is concerned with three things: location, location, location.

Developing a movie may or may not be getting involved with the world's greatest art form, but many will agree it is the art form offering the greatest possible range of artistic expression. The sound tracks are located to the left of each frame of film. There will likely be between eight and twenty-five sound tracks, probably an average of a dozen at any time during a movie. You, the scriptwriter, didn't write them all in your script—the unspoken ambience of your settings, the suggestibility of your words, the connotations of your expressions, and the finesse of your descriptions will suggest sounds to the editors and mixers and others at the final mix of the eventual movie, perhaps a year after it is photographed and three or four years after your script is written, maybe five or six years after you originally thought of the idea, which may have been inspired by a book you read or an event you witnessed ten years earlier.

THINKING IT THROUGH SO OTHERS MAY ACT ON IT

You may have thought long and hard about a particular location for action in your script—perhaps a city cellar where a rookie cop is coping with a conniving criminal. When the movie is made, your rookie becomes a veteran cop collaborating with a convicted cohort in a penthouse overlook. These things happen. Something else happens, too. Lots of what you've written never makes it to the final release print, for one reason or another.

You must work at getting a mood, timing and setting on your pages for experts to build upon. My guess is that people can get out of a chair one of a half-dozen different ways. An actor should increase those possibilities at least fourfold. The director or director of photography or producer may finally decide that the actor should jump down from a ladder rather than rise up from a chair. But if all goes well, the point of the shot, of getting your character, Joe, into the center of the room, still holds. He, however, ends up jumping into it. Why would a director bother to make such an insignificant change? Well, maybe the actor sprained his ankle during production; the director could shoot this shot with a double and establish that the character sprained his ankle when jumping off a ladder. Well, writers write stories, and scripts are always subject to change by whim or will.

Your original fifteen points should hold fast during all the winds of change on a location shoot, because, as an aggregate, they form the basis of the full story you want to film in ninety or so minutes.

Writers are generally not considered as talent by most movie people; writers, instead, are considered just below weed roots on any given movie talent roster. Writers—they are the ones who just serve to put thoughts and words into the minds and mouths of talented people, like dancers, singers, directors, and actors. A word of advice: The more they crave the glory, the more you, the writer, should covet the money. The proof is in the pudding: Walk down any street and ask anyone if they know who wrote *Gone With the Wind* or *Stagecoach* or *Citizen Kane* or *La Dolce Vita* or *The Maltese Falcon* or *Cabaret*—try it! You may turn to directing; it's a generally recognized talent.

As for writing, *most writers write because they have to. They drive themselves; writing means being read or heard, being published and paid.*

PICTURES IN ACTION

If you ever doubt the need to make action pictures in people's heads, just ask the next person you meet to tell you about any movie he or she saw recently. The response is likely to be as follows: The first thing they'll describe is an *action shot* or *scene*—a visual that moves, like the burning of Atlanta, when you inquire about *Gone With the Wind*. Second, if you ask, the person will make a stab at the story line, and probably give you the beginning and maybe the ending. Third, if you ask, you'll be told a little about the *different* characters. That's it, except for a brief, "I liked it" or "I didn't like it."

But the person probably won't be able to recall a single line of spoken dialogue—except on the rarest of rarest occasions. Movie dialogue is almost never quoted. Even then, it's likely to be a simple, perhaps pedestrian, line. So much for those who insist that movies are literary works. Like heck! Movies are visuals and sounds; words merely support the visual and other aural achievements, except for exposition, which is the revealing of facts through an exchange of dialogue.

Movies move at ninety feet a minute, three feet every two seconds, twenty-four frames a second. That's twelve times as fast as the fastest motor-driven still camera. Its speed is unrelenting. Every effort must be dedicated to keeping your movie moving ahead, to advancing characters, plot, and theme.

WIZARDS OF PHANTASM

Audiences want to escape from the literal world—facts, figures, notices, directional signs, instruction, education—into the figurative world. They want to get their worries right out of their heads. Movies deal with glamour, twaddle, poppycock, bosh, blather, humbug, fiddle-faddle, skimble-skamble, flummery, and trumped-up fantasies. People go to the movies to be entertained. Many seek relief in the womblike darkness of a movie theater, curling up in embryonic contortions and drowning themselves with popcorn and drinks. They're safe and sound again, bewitched by cinema conjurers who are enchanting them, beguiling them. Moviemakers are their wonderworkers, Wizards of Phantasm.

About 75 percent of moviegoers are between the ages of thirteen and twenty-nine. People fantasize more easily when they are young, healthy, and carefree. People over thirty years of age usually have problems they can't easily dismiss after a hard day at work. People over forty are somewhat more cynical about life; it's harder for them to fantasize as willingly as twenty-year-olds. Getting older can sometimes mean arthritis, rheumatism, bad backs, locking knees, weak and teary eyes. Sitting on one's rump for two hours and buying dreams on a silver screen, knowing there are real responsibilities to be dealt with at home is not all that easy. The aspiring screenwriter should keep these considerations in mind. Above all, you are writing a movie for youth, on the move, restless, and with all receptors reaching out for action. It was never any different.

I suggest that future filmmakers consider taking courses other than Drama 100, thereby enlarging their understanding of the world around them. Physics deals with matter and energy in terms of motion and force. Chemistry investigates composition and properties and changes. Physics and chemistry courses will do the prospective screenwriter more good than run-of-the-mill nonacademic courses, which are often nothing more than crapulous purblind drivel. Because so many prospective moviemakers dream of striking it rich, they should take some business courses and learn that a banker can be a human calculator strung together by glass eyes and steel valves beneath whose breast beats a gambler's heart. I would suggest that future writers take a year off from college and travel the world. Take two years, if you can. See and study the world and its people, file it all away in your brain and your notebooks. Eavesdrop on conversations. Join the longest lines wherever you are. Watch people, note and record every item on every wall. It's all future dialogue. One day, somewhere, somehow, you'll squeeze your brain and the whole darn thing will come pouring out and you'll set a scene and develop a narrative. It'll "feel" authentic on the screen.

To complement your personal observations, you should read at least two or three books a week. You might try carrying a paperback book of short stories everywhere you go. Read it when the going gets dull in a movie lobby, restaurant, graduation exercise, on the beach, in planes, and while waiting on line in the supermarket. It's a kind of forced intellectual ingestion; you've got to stuff yourself with information so that, one day, you'll put what you've seen together with what you've read and weld it with brains and creativity—the stuff that dreams are made of. *Study life, then study writing.* Get the content first, then the form; you'll be building from the inside out. That is the way to build a solid foundation.

ACTION SHOTS

How do we go about connecting shot to shot and scene to scene and sequence to sequence? How do we force the audience to pay attention to the story that's unfolding on the screen? After all, very few of them would sit on their duffs for two hours and read a book without getting up or wandering mentally. But scriptwriters do manage to keep an audience enthralled. And so will you. They do it with *nuances* and *hooks*. The best part of it is that audiences aren't aware of what's going on. Once you get into nuances and hooks, you'll never be able to see another movie without a greater sense of awareness and enjoyment. First off, you'll no longer be just a spectator in the audience, you'll be a participant. You'll be elbowing your friend sitting next to you, eager to point out each nuance, each hook, and what they mean. You'll enjoy it, but your neighbors won't—unless they know you want to write scripts. For that kind of ambition, they'll forgive almost anything. Remember? Writers get patted on the head, encouraged to do their thing because no one knows exactly what their "thing" is, so they figure they can't get hurt by it, whatever it is or may be.

Now that I've whetted your appetite for nuances and hooks, one fact should be noted before proceeding. When watching a play on a stage, audiences hear first and see second. It's the exact opposite with movie audiences. They see first, then hear; it's action before dialogue!

For example, here is a line of dialogue and a moment of action between Jane and Joe as it would be performed on stage:

JANE. "You bully!" [*Jane slaps Joe's face.*]

In the movies, it usually works like this:

JANE [*slapping Joe's face*]. "You bully!"

By writing action before dialogue, the scriptwriter can offer the actors, director, and editors the following alternatives:

1. The editors can cut the shot on Jane's slap as it hits Joe's cheek in a two-shot (two people in one shot) of Jane and Joe.
2. The editors can retain both the slap and the dialogue in a two-shot of Jane and Joe.
3. The editors can eventually print just the slap from Joe's point of view (a one-shot of Joe), omitting the dialogue.
4. The editors can eventually print just the slap from Jane's point of view (a one-shot of Jane), omitting the dialogue.
5. The editors may use both the slap and the line of dialogue but end the shot with Joe's reaction to being hit.
6. The editors may use the slap, the line of dialogue, Joe's reaction, and go a step further by ending the shot on Jane's reaction, to Joe's reaction.
7. The editors may use the slap, dialogue, Joe's reaction and Jane's reaction to Joe's reaction, and then two-shot to establish their mood about what they've just done, giving a hint as to what might happen next in their relationship.
8. The slap may not work on film; therefore, the shot may just consist of the line of dialogue.

There are many more possibilities for this shot. The point is that *the screenwriter helps the pacing of a movie by writing for action first, then dialogue.* The screenwriter also provides options to allow the director and editor to experiment with a variety of rhythms. Of course, it's wonderful to write for action and dialogue together, as a concomitant movement. It is best done when you know you are writing for known stars. As an independent, you just don't know who will be acting the parts you are writing. It is likely that the actors will be new or nearly new to the screen. Give them and their technicians the benefit of the doubt, and if the dialogue doesn't work, the shot can be cut on the initial action.

NUANCES AND HOOKS

You can't make movies without nuances. *A nuance is a characteristic repeated during the movie that advances the movie's action.* Suppose, for example, you are writing about a racing-car driver. He goes to a fabric store to buy silks. In the supply room, the salesgirl selects four bolts of silk: blue, green, red, and brown. On her way back to the counter, her boss helps her carry the load and offhandedly asks her who is interested in buying the silks. When she tells him a racing-car driver, he removes the green bolt (action before dialogue). Then he explains that green is a bad-luck color for racing drivers. Time passes in the movie and the driver we saw earlier, now dressed in blue, is in a race, whirling around the track. We see that the car in front of him has some green silk tied to its tail pipe. Well, that's a nuance. The screenwriter has telegraphed to the audience that something bad is going to happen to the driver of the racing car with the green silk on its tail pipe.

Let's try another example, one that may sound familiar. Suppose a character has been established as carrying an umbrella wherever he goes. Well, one sunny day he goes to a pawnshop, pawns something, and leaves. Now down the street, he realizes that he's forgotten his umbrella at the pawnshop. He returns and finds the shop empty, but spots his umbrella and picks it up. Turning to exit, he sees the pawnshop owner killing someone in the rear of the store. The Umbrella Man leaves in a hurry. What he doesn't know is that through a mirror the owner saw him witness the murder. So, the umbrella was the nuance. And the audience knows something that the Umbrella Man doesn't: The audience knows that the Pawnshop Man is going to go after the Umbrella Man, even though the latter, unaware that he's been seen, thinks himself safe. The audience is *involved* and *hooked*, too.

Setting up a nuance involves only the briefest screentime, whether it's done visually or verbally. It is a reasonable contrivance that works. It helps involve the audience and keeps attention focused on the story; it prevents the spectator's mind from wandering.

Nuances promote continuity. Some classic film nuances are in the briefcase of James Bond. We are quickly introduced to a series of gadgets and are told just what they are to be used for. We sit and wait for the time when each one of them will come in handy and help Bond get out of a tight situation. This is a prime example of how nuances can be used to integrate continuity into a script.

Hooks connect shots and scenes. They are the *connective tissues* in movies. It's nearly impossible to make a movie without hooks. And it's the writer's job to provide them. Without hooks, the audiences will not be able to follow your story. They won't connect with what's going on, on the screen.

The earliest game of "hooks" played by kids is called Geography. Remember it? It goes like this. One person says "Arkansas!" The next player names a geographical location beginning with the last letter of Arkansas. What the child is doing is hooking into, tagging, connecting, repeating. It hastens movement and keeps all the players on their toes, waiting and interested in seeing how the game will turn out. So, when the next kid says "San Salvador," he or she is followed by another who says "Rhode Island." Starting the next location with a first letter that matches the last letter of the previous location provides the connective tissue needed to keep the game going.

There are many types of hooks: verbal to verbal, verbal to visual, verbal to sound, visual to verbal, visual to visual, visual to sound, sound to visual, sound to sound, sound to verbal, and many other combinations.

Hooks can be used to reveal things that would otherwise take a considerable number of words to explain. For example: Suppose a father returns home at the end of a day's work and asks his wife where their son is. The wife replies that their son—whom we haven't yet seen on the screen—went to buy a new pair of shoes. The husband mumbles something to the effect that the kid bought a pair of shoes just a month or two ago. The wife defends the son by saying that growing, active boys wear out shoes very quickly. The husband replies that shoes are expensive. His wife says that their son read about a sale and she gave him $20. We then cut to the next shot, a teen-age boy in an alley with other boys. The teen-ager, who is the focus of our attention, is shooting craps (action before dialogue). He lays down a $20-dollar bill, cuffs the dice in his hands, and says, imploring the dice, "C'mon, bones, I need a new pair of shoes." We deduce from the above that: (1) The teen-ager is the son of the previously seen parents; (2) he's a liar; and (3) he's a gambler. The story has been connected and advanced and the character has been developed by hooking into the $20, which is a verbal-to-visual hook, and the word "shoes," which becomes a verbal-to-verbal hook. You have *revealed* facts through action, without stating or narrating them as you would in a documentary film. Another example of hooking is:

JOE. What's your movie about?
JESSIE. It's about ninety minutes.

The word "about" is the connective tissue. You have used eight words, but by repeating one word, the dialogue will sound like seven words and move faster. Let's try another one:

JOE. We can take in the Riviera and...
JESSIE.... and Venice and Lisbon and...
JOE.... the whole works, yes!

In this example we have used sixteen words, but note that the word "and" is used four times and the word "the" is used twice. So in this brief dialogue, *sixteen words will really sound like twelve words*. You've moved the dialogue faster and advanced the story as well. You can cut the shot on the word

"yes" and hook into the next shot of Joe and Jessie on a beach
with a sign nearby that reads "Welcome to the Riviera," making
for a verbal-to-visual hook.

Other visual-to-visual examples:

- Someone throws an orange; cut to a rising sun.
- A couple is finishing dinner; the guy lights his pipe and
smoke fills the screen. She says she'd like to take a trip to the
Rockies. He smiles, nods, and draws on his pipe, causing
more smoke. Cut to a railway station and smoke puffing
from a locomotive as the conductor calls out "all aboard for
Colorado." Without seeing the couple, we know they are
either on the train or about to board it.
- A surgeon, about to perform surgery, says to his nurse,
"This shouldn't take long—I have to be home early for
dinner." Cut to a woman in a butcher store asking the
butcher to cut three pounds of roast beef. He nods, slicing
into the meat. Well, she's the surgeon's wife, and if the
scene is done properly, the audience will relate to the
patient as the butcher draws blood from the beef.

Hooks cement. They link. They associate. For example,
remember the word-association game where someone says
"Snow" and the next person says "White." Or "Picture" and the
next person says "Frame" or "Perfect"—words that connect,
hook, complete, tag, and cement a thought. There are many TV
quiz games that use this device successfully.

Hooks close the gap. They provide closure to thoughts.

LET'S SUPPOSE

A screenwriter's world is full of supposes: Suppose you write a
screenplay...

> Will anyone buy it?
> If it is bought, will it become a movie?
> If it becomes a movie, will it be good enough to be
>   distributed?
> If it's distributed, will it do business?

If it does do business, will it also be reviewed?

If it is reviewed, will the critics discuss the script?

If they do discuss the script, will they have anything favorable to say about it?

Will producers, directors, stars, agents, investors, and studio heads recognize the writer and take an interest in your talent?

Suppose all this happens, will you turn out good scripts in the future?

Suppose you do just that? Then, more supposes.

While you're thinking about it, try these assignments to loosen up your thinking and keep you nimble about your budding craft.

1. Suppose you were given a wire coat hanger and asked how many uses you could think of for it? Start supposing and write down as many uses as you can for the next five minutes. Go! Try to get at least ten responses.

2. Suppose you start daydreaming, but as a learning exercise. Write a 250-word essay on daydreaming. Give yourself a time limit, say, thirty minutes or so.

3. Suppose you write a 250-word essay on old family photos. Make them come to life! Take thirty minutes.

4. Write an essay on the most interesting thing that has happened to you during the past six months. Define, describe, compare, and contrast the "happening" with other experiences. Why was this one unique? Be precise, strive for exactitude, knowing all along you'll be revealing your own preferences, values, and perceptions about life, simply by selecting this singular episode. Try for about 350 words in forty-five minutes of thinking and writing.

5. Suppose someone asked you to recommend some books to be read for pleasure and information? You'll likely suggest some with personal vigor, others strongly, still others mildly, and conclude your listing with various specialty books. Characterize and define the books, the stories, plots, themes, characters, authors. Differentiate

and delineate. Go to it, suggest a book list. Do it in about 500 words and take an hour to complete this exercise.

6. Write a two-minute speech about your favorite hobby. Try to write it in thirty minutes. Get started!

7. Write an essay on either Thanksgiving or Christmas. Focus in on at least six characters and interrelate them into a coherent group. Why are they there? What happens? About 350 words in forty-five minutes.

8. Write a 250-word essay on buying a car or bike or truck or anything that moves and carries at least one passenger. Involve at least three people. Take thirty minutes. Go!

9. Take a ride as a passenger in a friend's or relative's car. Take note of every signpost, light, storefront, pedestrian, driver, building, animal, and vehicle along the way. Then head back home to the typewriter and write an essay on observation—500 words with a beginning, middle, ending, resolution, and point of view. Take one hour.

10. Make a list of your favorite twenty-five movies and thereby enlighten yourself of your own personal preferences over the years. Have they changed? Are you changing?

It is important for beginning screenwriters to organize a body of work. Now is as good a time as any to get started. A good title for your writer's notebook might be: Once Upon a Time. This small suggestion seems to inspire aspiring scripters in many ways. Many of them begin to keep notes on each and every movie they see, with particular emphasis on just how the script did or didn't work and how they might have done better. Try it; it may get you into the groove of thinking in the language of screenwriting.

MORE SUPPOSES

• Suppose you could capture a cloud. How many uses could you make of it? Take fifteen minutes and see if you can come up with about twenty possibilities, both *literal* and *figurative*. One hitch, though. To complete this assignment properly, you should have a beginning, middle, and ending for each response. It's the only way to tell a story! (One of my students once responded immediately: "If I captured a cloud and brought it into this room, it would most assuredly cry and wet the floor. We'd all have to mop it up and I'd probably get my back out of joint, go to a hospital, and miss the rest of tonight's assignment." Well, that's a story!—and, a good response, too.)

- Script a two-minute scene with the following four characters: The Hunter, The Hunted, The Law, and The Rescuer. The Hunter could be the bounty hunter. The Hunted could be an escaped prisoner. The Law could be the sheriff. The Rescuer could be the Hunted's best friend. Take one hour.

- The Hamburger-Joint Scene (nearly every movie has one): It's when disparate characters meet and greet in a public place, such as a bar or restaurant or office, and as a result of the meeting, the movie develops new relationships and *the story leaps forward.* Think about the bar scene in *Star Wars*! Try your hand at a two-minute scene where a boy and girl meet at a burger joint and fall in love. This assignment will force you to think in terms of action and movement if you have each character arrive differently. Fill the location with at least three layers of action—foreground, middle, and background—interrelating your two principal characters with their environment. Take forty-five minutes.

- Write five one-minute scenes, integrating any two of the following into each minute: fear, discovery, friendship, betrayal, love, jealousy, revenge, rivalry, rage, loyalty. Take two hours.

- Conduct a one-minute interview with George Washington. Take thirty minutes.

- Describe the room you are in, in fifteen minutes; write no more than 200 words. After you've written this essay, ask yourself if you have defined, described, compared, and contrasted to the point where you've given a "personality" to the room. Have you built a scene with potential dramatic content?

CHAPTER 3

THE GOOD GUY AND THE BAD GUY

Generally, all the major characters in your script should appear during the first ten minutes of the movie. In no case should they appear later than twenty minutes into the film.

The Good Guy and the Bad Guy should each make their initial appearance no later than the first ten minutes of your movie—the sooner the better. *The theme of your movie should be revealed during the first three to five minutes.* How do you reveal the theme? You'll probably do it visually, not with words. You'll have one or two action shots, each dealing with the theme. For example, if your movie is science fiction, the theme is almost surely to be man's loss of freedom. So right at the start show a person or some people who are losing, or are likely to lose, personal control over their lives.

As a writer, you must jump right into the task of revealing lead characters, theme, and story. If you don't grab the audience's attention at the beginning, *when they are most receptive*, you'll lose them, never to recover their interest.

PERSONAL PRONOUNS

Most beginning scriptwriters get bogged down in personal pronouns and names. For example:

JOE. I mean we should be together, just you and me, Jessie.

JESSIE. Yes, Joe, just we two. We need each other, you and I.

JOE. I'm glad you said that, Jessie.

JESSIE. Well, Joe, I mean it. It's just you and me.

JOE. I like it that way, Jessie, just us.

JESSIE. Joe, you put things so well.

JOE. That's because we mean a lot to each other.

JESSIE. I'm glad you said that. I like it and I like you, Joe.

Well, that's *deadly dull*. It's script form but it isn't scriptwriting. Yet, most beginners go through it, and they've got to overcome it. You'll never succeed if you write it that way.

A better example might be:

JOE. From now on we're a team.

JESSIE. What's my position?

JOE. Play it my way and we'll be partners.

JESSIE. Okay, partner...

CONFLICT

The people who will go to see your movie grew up on television. They expect something to happen every six to eight minutes. On television, it's a commercial, a message. In movies, the message is action. We discussed earlier the suggestion that your movie should be fifteen sequences of about six to eight minutes each. It's a rhythm that movie audiences expect after a lifetime of TV watching. Pace your action, but get into the rhythm of writing about a confrontation, crisis, sharp tension—action, filmic action—every six to eight minutes. Of course, that's easier said than done. *Most people back away from tension and problems in real life. It's even harder to write about.* In fact, it's one of the most difficult things to handle in screenwriting, because it is inherently melodramatic, like making a mountain out of a molehill. It's a theatrical exaggeration. It means dealing with conflict. An inability to handle it precludes otherwise talented people from succeeding at screenplay writing.

Here are some brief suggestions to warm you up to the task of handling certain types of conflict and creative possibilities in screenplays:

- Write a one-minute action scene about an accident in which someone dies.
- Write a one-minute action scene about a fire in which someone is badly burned.
- List as many uses you can for a junked automobile. Take ten minutes. Try to come up with fifteen answers.

ACTION

Another problem beginners face is how to describe action. *Never* write: They talk or sit or walk or get up or pull a car into a driveway or leave or look or stare. Instead of having your character stare, define the stare. Is it a leer? Is your character spying or catatonic or peering? Say it exactly! Ditto for all the rest: Define and describe in just one or two words the manner in which the character is talking or sitting or getting up. When a car arrives on a scene, describe its locomotion and appearance in words that connote visuals and sounds. Have the car chug, screech, squeal, or clang—it sure beats writing that the car pulled into the driveway. The reason you are a writer is because you have the ability to *describe* the action precisely. Stay in tune with the sights, sounds, shapes, and colors you want to convey.

USE OF COLOR

The use of color in screenplays is another method of introducing dialogue. For example, purple or navy blue will suggest a *foreboding* of things to come later in the movie. They are good colors to enhance the mood of a mystery or psychological suspense. On the other hand, bright red or kelly green can be effective in a straight out-and-out action flick, like a monster epic.

DIALOGUE CUTAWAY

Another trick to increase suspense is the dialogue cutaway. For example:

> JOE [*to Jessie*]. [*Joe twists Jessie's arm.*] Where's Jim?
> JESSIE [*grimacing tearfully*]. He's...
> [CUT TO: *Jim lurking behind a holly bush outside the house that Joe and Jessie are in.*]
> [CUT TO: *Joe dragging Jessie downstairs inside the house.*]
> JOE. *Okay, point him out.*
> [CUT TO: *Jim rising from behind the bush outside the house.*]

Will Jessie walk out the door of the house and put the finger on Jim? Did Jessie spill the beans? What did she tell Joe? If she doesn't point out Jim, where will she lead Joe?—on a wild goose chase or to a spot where Jim can overcome Joe and rescue Jessie?

Dialogue cutaways keep the audience guessing and advance the story while creating action and revealing character.

DOING IT

How does one go about the physical act of screenwriting? Some writers insist on using pencils, many with a specific brand or lead hardness. Others like a dozen sharp pencils near them. Still others cannot write in longhand. They maintain they can only think while typing. And then there are those who dictate, have everything transcribed by a typist, and then revise in ink. Many writers struggle all day, while some only work in the morning. Others function best while pacing or dreaming. You'll just have to experiment and discover what suits you best. Whatever you choose, you'll have one thing in common with most other screenwriters: You'll procrastinate. You'll eat an apple, take a nap, go for a walk. You'll look for any excuse to avoid facing another empty page or a filled one that's shouting at you for necessary editing. Laziness goes with the territory. You're not alone, but you'll never make it unless you develop the habit of writing every day or at least think about and make notes about your characters. If you do develop a working rhythm and then break it, you'll find it hard to get back into a routine. There are probably only a thousand screenwriters or so in all the world. If you want to enter their world you'll have to be as unique as they are. That kind of uniqueness means talent, knowing your craft and working at it constantly and diligently. There are many people who call themselves screenwriters, but no one else thinks they are. *A screenwriter is someone who is paid for screenwriting.*

CREATIVE USE OF
AVAILABLE RESOURCES

You can help yourself to an abundance of study materials. For example, scan your weekly TV guide. What movies are scheduled to be broadcast? Write down the titles, go to the library, see if you can get the scripts. If not, there may be paperbacks in secondhand bookshops with adapted scripts. Buy them. Then go to your local library, to the shelf marked "791." You'll see lots of movie books. Some of them might have some criticism of the films you're about to watch on television. Armed with learning aids, you can watch the movie, follow the script, and, afterwards, read some criticism about it. All it takes is about two hours and it's both peaceful and rewarding. *You should see at least three movies every week during the period you're learning about screenwriting.*

TIMELY TIP

Treat yourself to a stopwatch. If you want to be a screenwriter, you'll need a stopwatch the way an adman needs a ruler, to measure, not by the inch but by the second, because you'll be measuring time. Screentime. Use your stopwatch to time different shots on every movie you go to until you're as good as a jockey at judging pace. A jockey can work out a horse according to the instructions of his trainer, who might tell him to let the steed run four furlongs (½ mile) in 48 and 1/5 seconds. You can bet that the jockey, if he wants to keep his job, will follow the trainer's orders and bring that horse back to the barn after running without any variance or, at most, 1/5 of a second. Like the jockey, you're going to have to carry a clock in your head if you intend to understand the meaning of a well-paced script. It must become second nature to you, and if you apply yourself to the problem, you'll develop the knack. Don't go to Hollywood without it.

WRITE YOUR REVIEW

Do you really think your idea for a movie will work? Reserve judgment until you've tried this assignment on for size: Write four paragraphs—the kind that might be written by the movie critic of a major daily newspaper—reviewing your movie. Write your "review" in this order: opening paragraph, last paragraph, second paragraph, and next-to-last paragraph.

Your opening paragraph will discuss WWWWWH: Who, What, When, Where, Why, and How.

Your last paragraph will sum up everything you want to say about the film.

Your second paragraph will probably discuss the story, plot, theme, timeliness, aptness; generally, the second paragraph will most likely include a value judgment about the script, the genesis of the movie.

Your next-to-last paragraph will reveal the shortcomings of the movie: what the writer intended it to be and how it could have been written better. (You're free also to criticize the director and the actors.)

The above device is an effective way for a writer to analyze the idea that is screaming to be filmed. It's like the old saw about asking a person's age and then asking for one thought for each year, like, "Let's have 39 thoughts on being 39." Writing the review of your movie before you've written the script makes sense; I suggest you try it for your latest and best script idea. Take an hour to do it; it's not as easy as it seems.

Another device to test your story idea is to tell it to a stranger—its beginning, middle, ending, and resolution—in three to four minutes. Watch the expression on the face of your listener. Is the person getting sleepy? Are you eliciting expected responses? After you've told your story, ask your listener to repeat it to you. What with the inevitable changes the other person makes, how does it sound to you? In "playing" it back to you, the other person will likely emphasize the parts he or she liked, verbalizing that selective retention.

These devices are intended to get the writer out of his or her own subjectivity. They are fairly reliable and rather objective learning techniques for aspiring screenwriters. Try them.

GHOSTS

Some actors help create their lines as the scene unfolds; sometimes for an entire movie. For example, *Casablanca* is reputed to have been made that way. But most often there was an original screenwriter and maybe one to ten script "doctors" who revised the script—producers, directors, actors, investors, friends, relatives, and the professionals. Everybody gets in the act!—*only because almost no one likes the original screenplay.* Everybody is a script judge, qualified or not. Learn to expect this. You'll just have to get used to the fact that writers are people for hire. The names of many scriptwriters are never flashed on the screen; they are paid cash while others reap the credit. It's the way the world turns, especially for beginners and employees of established scripters. The latter keep their mouths shut because they are paid well and weekly. They are "ghosts," just like those in all other areas of commerce, industry, and politics.

STAY TUNED FOR THE NEXT SHOW

If your screenplay ever becomes a movie and you want to spend your time productively, see the movie, then stay for the next show. But this time move down to the front row on one side and look back at the audience as the movie is projected once more. You'll hear the words and music and effects again, associating them with specific visuals. Only now you'll be noting the facial reactions and body language of patrons moving in, out of, up and around their seats. Are the responses you see the ones you expected when you wrote your script? If you're not connecting with audiences, go to a newsstand and buy a large and varied supply of teen-age magazines. Study the ads and see what teen-agers are buying. In your active pursuit of knowledge about the people you're writing about, listen to all those radio and television programs that teen-agers like. Doing these things regularly can provide a type of survival-and-prosperity insurance for screenwriters because they keep you alert and attuned to the society—youth—that you're writing your movies for.

GET A GRIP ON YOUR OWN THOUGHTS

One of my former students, a dentist, told his fellow classmates that he was finding it difficult to look into patients' mouths without thinking, "cut, dissolve, and wipe." He was referring, of course, to the traditional methods of moving from shot to shot in a script. I am forever surprised by the varying backgrounds of people who want to study screenwriting. They are all well educated. Why are they now interested in screenwriting? Is it part of the rush toward continuing education? Perhaps. In profiling my students I have discovered that most are either working for the common good or for someone else's global goal or to make some boss look better. Screenwriting students seem to share a desire to learn a craft where they can do something personal, enjoy it as a learning experience, and maybe profit from their own individual efforts.

The best of them work by the "inches," so to speak. *They realize that writing is really rewriting* and they get right into it. They speak about their characters as if they were alive, yet, for all their fantasizing, handle them prudently and reasonably, however contradictory that may sound. They press their characters into situations that force twists and turns in plotting, as if they were moving them on a chessboard. The worst students, however, study script after script in Proustian detail, like bookkeepers, hoping to unlock the secrets of scripting just by reading major scripts. What they fail to do is reason for themselves, think for themselves, explore the dimensions of their own stories. They see scripts and movies only with stars and stardust in their eyes, blind to the need to pursue hard work on their own. By not writing and rewriting, they fail to come to grips with their own thoughts and words.

IT'S A LONG WAY TO TIPPERARY

To enter the world of scripting, it helps to be a romantic. To think that your script will become a work of art, created by artisans, professionals and other people of the craft, called a movie, a multimillion-dollar effort, to be viewed by millions of audiences around the world is, let's face it, a romantic notion. If you ever find the script that you began on a yellow-lined pad at your desk turns out to be a movie that you get to see in a theater while on vacation in France or Italy or Japan or Australia, you'll know the feeling at once. A dream come true—a romantic notion indeed.

CHAPTER 4

WRITING TO ORDER

Earning a living by doing something you like to do is really something of a miracle. You have one thing going for you. You are a specialist! It's time consuming and it demands all your attention. The other things generalists generally have going for them preclude devotion to a single assignment. Okay, so you are a specialist, so what? There are lots of them. Agents receive constant requests for the screenwriting services of their leading clients, the writers who already have track records. A track record means the writer has written movie and TV scripts and, usually, novels, novellas, and short stories, as well. There is a constant demand for their services.

If a beginning screenplay writer sells his or her first effort as a TV movie of the week, the fee might range from $7,500 to $15,000, whereas a veteran writer will receive $35,000 to $45,000. You are unproven. The veteran writer will probably be solicited by the producer and asked to write; you won't be invited. You've got to sell yourself and your budding, willing talent. If you are serious about it, approach a producer with some scripts you've already written. After reading your work, he or she might decide that none of it is suitable but that your talent is real and available. Seize the moment by creating an opportunity—try to get a two- or three-week writing assignment, any kind, to show your stuff, to prove you can write to order. If there is any kind of honest intent on the part of the producer and he or she has a property or two that needs developing, he or she might just consider your offer. It's a start!

Veteran screenwriters working on major motion pictures receive anywhere from $50,000 to $500,000 for their scripts. Many receive fees in the $100,000 to $200,000 range. That's for starters, because they are likely to receive contingencies and/or deferrals and/or points, all of which we will tackle a little later in this book. They are accomplishers. You, on the other hand, are a tyro, an aspirer. Like the producers who have to sell themselves to established writers, you have to sell yourself to producers. It's far from easy. Their offices are cluttered with screenplays stacked tall, like telephone directories.

People who receive unsolicited manuscripts almost always return them, unopened, to the sender. There is a solid reason for this action by the addressee. If the manuscript is read, and if anything from that script is ever found in a future movie made by the addressee, the fear is that the sender might sue the makers of the movie for stealing his or her material. To avoid this possibility, however remote, scripts are returned unread. A script offered by a registered agent, however, receives a different reception. So, be on notice: Get yourself an agent. The Catch 22 is that you must first write a polished, professional screenplay. The cost of typing a script can be $300. Scripting is an expensive undertaking, not only in time but in terms of money as well.

Okay, you've got that good first script. Find an agent to handle your work. It's hard enough to be both a creative writer and objective editor. Why risk being a salesperson and businessperson as well? Most creative people are lousy negotiators. They just want their work shown and seen, sometimes at any cost to them. Screenwriters and financial advisers don't even speak the same language; the former's world is scripts, the latter's, balance sheets; one thinks in terms of words, the other, numbers. So, a buffer between you and a prospective buyer is recommended.

Let's hope you get to the point where an agent agrees to take you on as a client. The usual fee for services, contingent on making a deal for you, is 10 percent, and the agent will probably ask for an exclusive contract to sell your script, plus twenty-four months to accomplish the task, which should be fine with you.

You now have an agent. Lo and behold, the agent snares a buyer who wants to option your screenplay. When someone options a screenplay he or she buys the exclusive right to try to develop your script for a certain period of time, usually one year. You receive payment—say $2,000 less 10 percent to the agent—for selling this option. At the same time that your agent is negotiating the option, you will enter into a conditional sales contract, defining the terms of the sale if the party who is optioning your script decides to buy it during the year. If he or she does decide to buy, you may get another $13,000 to $23,000, bringing the total up to the $15,000 to $25,000 range, which is a reasonable beginning price. This isn't gospel and there are extremes both downward and upward. You'll have lots of decisions to make. If, on the other hand, the party who optioned your script decides not to buy it, you keep the original $2,000 and the script is your property once again. Let's suppose, however, that the party who optioned your script, does decide to buy it.

The buyer will know it's your first effort and how important it is for you, both psychologically and professionally, to get your name up on a screen. The buyer probably genuinely believes that your script can be turned into a successful movie, and there is a meeting of minds. You and the buyer both "see" your screenplay as a commercial film, but—a word of caution. Try to evaluate the buyer's *ability* to turn your script into a movie. One buyer who has a 100 percent or even 80 percent chance of producing the film may offer you less money than a buyer who has only a 20 percent or even 50 percent chance of seeing the film completed. Consider taking less money. There are no sure things, of course, but the elimination of as many obstacles as possible in the long journey from script to screen is a plus.

STEP BY STEP

Suppose your agent calls you with the happy news that someone is interested in having you write an original screenplay. The offer probably surfaced because your agent showed your scripts to someone who was impressed with your skills. You'll likely be offered a step deal. The contract for the script might be $25,000, payable in steps, perhaps as follows:

> Step 1. You write a 50-page treatment
> and receive $2,500,
> half now and half on delivery.

If the buyer doesn't want to continue for any reason, he or she then owns the treatment, you keep the $2,500, and the contract ends, period. If the buyer elects to continue, the next step is:

> Step 2. You write a first-draft screenplay
> and receive $7,500,
> half now and half on delivery.

Again, if the buyer, after receiving your first draft, doesn't want to continue for any reason, the contract ends. He or she owns everything and can do with it what he or she wants when he or she wants. You, on the other hand, keep the $7,500. However, if the buyer elects to continue, the next step is:

> Step 3. You write a second draft of the screenplay
> and receive $7,500,
> half now and half on delivery.

If the buyer decides to continue, the next step is:

> Step 4. You write a first revision of the screenplay
> and receive $3,500,
> half now and half on delivery.

If the buyer decides to continue—and I want to emphasize that it's his or her decision alone; it is not only the buyer's unilateral right to stop the step-by-step process whenever he or she wants to but he or she also owns all the material you've provided thus far. The next step is:

Step 5. You write a second revision of the screenplay
and receive $2,000,
half now and half on delivery.

If the buyer elects, there is a final step:

Step 6. You write a polish of the screenplay
and receive $2,000
half now and half on delivery.

The above description is a basic working guide. There may be
more or less money involved, there may be more or fewer steps.
It is essential for you to secure immediately the services of a
qualified attorney who deals in this kind of contract. Your agent
will offer you industry advice and your attorney will provide you
with legal advice, but the final decision—the business decision—
is yours alone. The time will come when you receive bona fide
offers. When that happens, you'll have a lot to think about other
than the "people and places" in your first script. Many writers
think about taking a vacation or having a champagne party.
Likely, you'll just pay some old bills and start your next script or,
at least, start thinking about it. Consistency is the mark of a
professional; it's what distinguishes a pro from an amateur. *A
professional attitude also means people can rely on you to do
what you say you can do.* Amateurs talk a lot and write little. Pros
talk less but write a lot. Writers are paid to write, not talk.

BE REASONABLE

To have a better chance of selling your first script, keep
production costs in mind. Write a script that can be produced for
from $400,000 to $1 million. Let's face it, you aren't going to be
asked to write a big-budget, major motion picture. You aren't a
phone call away from some studio head asking for your services
on the next $5 million feature. To prepare for this initial sale, see
all current PG- and R-rated movies, such films as *The Black Hole,
Apocalypse Now, Unmarried Woman, Star Wars, The Deer
Hunter, Coming Home, Superman,* and others—*all* those low-
budget action flicks that so many people look down their noses
at.

All those horror, sci-fi, gangster, and teen-age movies are learning experiences. The aspiring writers who don't see and learn from them are doomed to failure and a life of talking about how bad movies are, and how much better they could have done, if they wanted. Those people make their deals in the air, not on paper the way contracts are really written.

Accountants see *all* clients. Lawyers see *all* clients. Physicians see *all* patients. Why should you be different? If you consider yourself above it all, forget about screenwriting.

SCREENWRITING TIPS

Watch those crowd scenes in your scripts. To assemble 100 extras for a 30-second shot will cost between $2,500 and $6,000 just for them. In addition, the budget will include set decoration, costumes, lighting, and so on. Animals, animal trainers, special vehicles, a unique kind of weather, an unusual location, stunts, major equipment, and extra cameras can increase costs tenfold. It's advisable to price the costs of your script every ten pages or so. You don't want the budget for your script to price you out of a sale. Union grips—people who do manual labor (three to five on every movie)—each earn about $700 a week. If four grips are necessary on location for a four-week shoot, budget $11,200 for their salaries, plus additional costs for housing, food, and travel for twenty-eight days. The typical crew size for a movie budgeted at around $750,000 will number about thirty-five. Grips get the *least* money. That does not include your actors' salaries, food, housing, and transportation costs. To give your script the best chance of becoming a film, pay close attention to costs, however noncreative you may view the effort. We will deal with this in Part 2: Production.

SCREENWRITING:
ONCE UPON A TIME

Once upon a time...

...a kid grows up on a farm, falls in love with cars, becomes a dirt-track racer, and gets a shot at the big time.

...a couple of convicts escape from prison.

...a creature from the depths of the sea appears over the crest of a wave

...an unrequited love drives a mad scientist to evil deeds.

...a stranger with strange ways rides into a quiet prairie town.

...a deadly, top-secret drug falls into enemy hands.

...a truckers' association decides once and for all to make a concerted effort to stop hijacking.

...a band of renegade Indians pursue westward settlers.

...a long-lost letter is delivered.

...four college buddies decide to spend the summer working at a health fair.

Try your skills at adding a middle, ending, and resolution to each of the above ten items, but in no case add more than 100 words to any of your responses. Be succinct. Less is more.

Less is more! You don't want to turn in a 250-page script for your ninety-minute movie when you need only 90 to 120 pages to get the job done. Make every second count or you won't get a second chance to show your talents—more or less.

WRITING AND
TALKING TO WRITERS

Who can screenwriters talk to about their craft? Where should they live? Where can they meet other screenwriters and feel comfortable about being with a group of people who don't consider budding screenwriters as pariahs or oddballs with a strange "hobby"? Do you have to live in New York or Los Angeles? These are some of the questions that starting scripters have. If you are thinking about or asking these kinds of questions, you are thinking seriously about your work and seeking a creative milieu in which to function and grow. Try your imagination. Write to screenwriters. Where are they? They're up on the screen for about three or four seconds. Take down their names. Write to them in care of the network or studio that produced their script. They'll probably be surprised and delighted to hear from you, especially if you have a kind word to say, and ask them for a copy of their script. You'll probably get one too.

Are there any writers' clubs or organizations in your area? Try the phone book or a nearby college. Head for the library and make a list of your favorite contemporary authors. Write to them at their publishing houses. Remember, the writers you contact were once in your position. Somewhere along the line someone probably gave them a helping hand; they may return the favor. If you approach them properly, most writers will not only talk to you, they'll spill the beans for you. After all, you may be their only direct link with immortality and the glory they associate with the silver screen.

Another possibility for striking up friendships with people who have similar interests to yours is in continuing education courses, perhaps even a program granting an advanced degree. Competing with adults who are highly motivated should sharpen your observational acuity and hone your budding skills. By meeting deadlines, reading and comprehending lengthy assignments, and competing with your peers, you'll experience a kind of forced self-discipline. It may just fit the bill as part of your prescription for success, a scenario fit for an achieving writer.

GOOD-BYE SCENARIO, HELLO CINEMA

Your characters are individualized by the clothes they wear, the apartments they live in, the way they travel, the tempo of their talk, and the kind of work they do. Your aim is to make the audience understand your personal vision of some characters you had rolling around in your mind and decided to write about. Concentrate your efforts on directing your characters; leave the directing of camera angles to the person directing the movie. Once your script has been turned into a shooting script, the director usually doesn't go near it. He or she has memorized the script and the story that he or she wants to tell. Everyone's effort is directed toward the making of the movie. The script no longer has a life of its own. It is now in the process of becoming a movie. Your job is done. It's good-bye scenario, hello cinema! But don't be too depressed. It only happens to the best of people—those whose scripts become movies.

CRYSTAL-BALLING THE 1980S

Predictions for the 1980s:

1. *The script will be written from the point of view of the camera.* The writer will be the camera. This differs substantially from novels where the point of view is usually the major character. Producers will more and more insist on writers who have a *visual* comprehension of the ultimate product. The natural consequence of that demand will make the producer's job relatively effortless. The producer's constant search for ways to reduce reliance on directors to visualize a script, to give it a "look" that it doesn't inherently have, will be ended when the script itself visualizes—in short, when scripts "see" and make producing a movie a simpler task.

2. *Producers will want scripts in polished form.* No longer will they be willing to judge a script on its first, second, third, or even fourth draft. They will want to read a polished script, ready to produce. This means the writer will have to produce a script that is closer to a shooting script rather than a basic screenplay. The job of writer will be to render a screenplay without spelled-out angles but with angles and camera movement inherent in the action. Simply put, it means that scripts will become leaner and leaner. Less and less will mean more and more. Writers will be forced to use words that suggest not only sounds and action but camera movement as well. Writers will be paid handsomely for their efforts.

3. *There will be a renaissance for writers in the 1980s.* The demand for finished, fully-polished screenplays will

increase dramatically. *Scriptwriting will be the liveliest profession in Hollywood.*

4. *Scriptwriters will be in greater demand as producers and/or directors.* Therefore, learn everything you can about making a film *before* you begin writing in earnest. Take courses in production, acting, and directing. Learn how to work a camera, understand lighting. Work in a film lab and learn just what happens to film, how you can work with film and make it work for you to get the exact image, mood, and feeling that you want. One day, if someone wants to make a movie of your script, you may end up directing and producing it as well!

WAKE-UP EXERCISES

Here are some screenwriters' wake-up exercises for those idle moments during the next week or two:

1. Early one morning a group of men go duck hunting. Write a three-minute scene from the point of view of the ducks. Take an hour. Make your point clear visually, develop characters, advance the story, and, maybe, get a laugh. There must be a beginning, middle, ending, and resolution, of course, along with your message.

2. Joe, a teen-age descendant of Attila the Hun, meets Jessie, a teen-age descendant of Florence Nightingale, one sunny Sunday at Disneyland. They fall in love, then discover each other's identities. What happens? Script a three-minute scene. Reveal who they are, don't state it. And again, you'll need a point to the scene and a storyline. Take two hours.

3. A vagrant on a park bench is given $1 million in cash and told that if he spends it within one hour he'll be handed another gift of $2 million. Write a 250- to 300-word essay. What happened? To whom? What? Where? Why? When? How? Make pictures with words and keep your story moving, fast. Take forty minutes.

4. A 50-foot pleasure craft with twenty guests on board for a day's outing 10 miles offshore springs a leak. What happens? Why? What happens as a result of something else happening? Who's the Good Person? The Bad Person? The Crazy Person? The Rational Person? Bring something unexpected into the scene. Try your hand at establishing, developing, and advancing characters. Write a two- to two-and-a-half-minute scene. Take two hours.

5. A huge rocket falls from space and lands in an open field. Something's in it. What? And something happens. What? Use at least three characters in scripting a one- to one-and-a-half-minute scene with nuances and foreboding as if you were scripting a sci-fi movie. Take an hour and a half. Think figuratively while trying to suggest a sense of reality in a fantasy situation.

6. A cub reporter bursts into his city editor's office and tells her that he's hot on the trail of some local crime lords. The city editor orders the cub reporter to drop his investigation and spend the next two weeks in the office editing obituaries. Write the next minute of the movie. Use at least three characters. What happens? End the scene with a hint or two about what will happen next. Take forty-five minutes to work on this exercise.

7. For additional exercises to tune up your writing skills, as well as for an excellent set of pointers on developing your overall writing ability, consult *Finding Yourself in Print: A Guide to Writing Professionally*, by Dr. Riley Hughes of Georgetown University. Published by New Viewpoints, a division of Franklin Watts.

PART 2

PRODUCTION

CHAPTER 5

MOVIES AND THE ASPIRING INDEPENDENT

Movies are made for money. Making movies is an expensive business. The quickest route into the industry is to be born rich, marry rich, or have access to unlimited credit.

Every movie requires a lot of cash. Real dollars. Not wish fulfillments; you just can't wish your way into financing. Let's face it, you're an Independent. In this business an Independent is a person who is:

...out of work

...thinking about making a movie after college

...wondering whether he or she should consider a career change, maybe make a movie

...a "filmmaker" without enough money to (1) pay a lawyer to write a proposal and (2) buy film to shoot a movie

...ready to direct his or her first film after having taken two film courses

...confident that working with an accountant on a budget breakdown will sap his or her creative energies

...promoting himself or herself as a moviemaker after piecing together an out-of-focus 8mm or 16mm short subject, which won an escutcheon award at a pyrrhic film festival and reeks of the word amateur

...promising to invest $15,000 in a movie if he or she gets the job of associate producer and is advised that the title associate producer usually *sells* for $25,000, plus one proviso: He or she disappears while the movie is being made

...fired from a film crew because of his or her constant whispering about how wrong the director and cameraman are in rehearsing the actors and in setting up the shots—and worse, is blackballed from the industry for life by the producer, a legal right that can be exercised, with cause, under certain circumstances.

...flying by the seat of his or her pants.

You might say there's more to movies than initially meets the eye of the aspiring independent.

The ten major motion-picture producing-distributing companies are only releasing between seventy-five and 100 new movies annually. That's all! The next twenty or so companies combined—a few major-minors but mostly minor-minors— release another 100 or 200 general-audience movies annually. That's the movie business! Where do you fit in? Let's budget that movie of yours.

PREPRODUCTION, PRODUCTION, POSTPRODUCTION

An independent, low- to medium-budget film may take eight months of preproduction time, four to six weeks of production time on location, and another eight months of postproduction time. You may end up with 100 hours of effort for each minute of eventual screentime in your finished movie. And, true time, the number of manhours when multiplied by those 100 hours? Well, you can see that it's all very time consuming and dependent on the talented efforts of a large number of people sharing the same vision. Indeed, it is a group effort with a single goal: making an entertaining movie that will make money.

LEARN TO PLAN BY DOING

Detailed planning is essential to both the experienced and inexperienced filmmaker. The same kinds of problems must be faced on every shoot even though each film is a unique enterprise. To learn how to plan, get a job on the set of one or two movies. You'll gain enough experience to overcome the beginner's feeling of greenness.

YOUR $750,000 MOVIE

A major company "look" is a reasonable goal, because you may ultimately offer it to one of the ten majors for distribution. If you try to enlist the attention of these distributors, you'll be competing with the biggest and best studio films. They're going to judge your film against many others. Los Angeles screening rooms are stacked with those heavy metal film cans, each one containing a completed movie that wasn't sold. They lie there year after year collecting dust, because their owners were not able to sell them. Nobody wants them. Their owners most likely ran out of cash and didn't have the money to ship them home. If there's any "heart" in the movie industry, those screening-room projectionists have it. They make sure the film is ready to go back to the owner, who may someday make a comeback and retrieve his or her goods—the film that 100 or more people worked on, only to see their dreams dissolve. And the gray, 30-pound film cans? They sit there like tombstones, monuments to broken hearts. But your film isn't going to end up that way. Your film is going to come home a winner.

To be a winner, however, you must first understand that success means *interdependence* not independence, in the complicated world of film production. So many film students want to be writer-director-producer *in their first job*. Please subordinate that kind of ego. Be modest like the rest of the interdependent movie crowd. They've paid their "dues." They long ago discovered the need for interdependence.

BUDGETING YOUR $750,000 MOVIE

A budget is composed of two parts: above the line and below the line. The items listed above the line are nonvariable. Each item has a fixed negotiated cost, settled by contract, prior to production.

Above-the-line costs include: story and screenplay, producer and staff, associate producer and staff, director and staff, lead actors, supporting actors, and extras.

Story and Screenplay

A reasonable cost for the story, screenplay, script "doctoring," typing, and Xeroxing copies is always difficult to arrive at. You are the one buying it. From your point of view, you'll be bargaining as best you can for the cheapest price for the very best script you can get. The writer may ask for $15,000 or even $25,000. You may offer $10,000 on a take-it-or-leave-it basis. The writer may say he or she will take your offer provided that he or she gets 1 percent of the profits of the movie. Well, you'll be doing what you must—making decisions—throughout the production. Let's suppose you counter offer ½ percent and that the writer agrees. You've struck a deal. Now you know your first cost above the line is $10,000 plus ½ percent of the profits, if any.

You will have to define the word "profit" in a legal sense. Your attorney and the writer's attorney will work it out.

With the cost of the story and script out of the way, you'll be concentrating on the costs of reworking the screenplay. You'll probably hire some "ghosts" to refine it to your satisfaction. Figure another $2,000 for this item. Next, the costs of typing and copying forty copies for cast and crew of a 100-page script will cost roughly $400. Total for the first above-the-line expense: $12,400.

Producer and Staff

A "creative producer," which means a "working producer," stays with the project from the beginning to the end—from the time the script is bought through all the preproduction planning, principal photography, and postproduction work, including editing, timing (the lighting of the print), scoring, mixing, and selling the finished product to a distributor.

In our hypothetical budget, let's strike a bargain with this producer. Your contract with him or her will probably cover at least a year's work, maybe more. Figure eighteen months. Figure a total salary of $36,800. Of course, if your producer has already made a couple of films, the price will almost assuredly be higher. In addition to the cash, you'll probably work out some kind of incentive arrangement, a percentage of the profits, if any. Try 2½ percent. It is a reasonable amount, for it is the producer alone who is involved on a day-to-day basis with the making of your movie. A better word for producer would be orchestrator. In the early days of the business there was no such job title as producer. They were called supervisors. Your producer will need part-time and full-time help. Figure $15,400. Total for the second above-the-line expense: $52,200.

Associate Producer and Staff

This is a good job for you. You raised the money. You want to be your own producer *someday*, don't you? Your salary? How about $16,400? Why so little? Because you're the boss and you own the greatest possible share of the movie and are the sole person in the entire organization who stands to benefit the most. As for a staff, well there's nothing in the budget to cover the cost of such a luxury. You want to put every available dollar to work making a better movie, don't you? Sure you do. So, share the producer's staff, when they're not busy, of course. Cost for this item: $16,400.

Director and Staff

Now you're into "talent." You're seeking a director who can, primarily, work with actors—rehearse them, inspire them, get them to think and move and act at the same time. You'll also want a director whose vision of the movie is the same as yours. Some directors can be a bit perverse and work at cross-purposes with their employers. You'll also have to settle on just who has creative control over the movie. I suggest you keep it. Don't give it to the director. Don't make the director an executive with boardroom privileges about the way your movie will look. You'll have the responsibility of selling the film. The investors will hold you accountable. Remember that. You've got to stand on your own two feet. Now's the time. Creative control over everything in the movie is yours! The director directs talent and does his or her other things, like knowing how and when to call for sound and camera and lighting and how to frame a picture so it becomes a part of a coherent whole. The best directors are concertmasters. They get an individual, unique sound out of their performers. Each concertmaster gets a different sound, and so does a good director.

Realizing that there will one day be a sum total—a movie—and that the sum total will be greater than its parts, you will want a director with a holistic approach. The search for a director is usually made by the producer, associate producer and production manager (whom we will discuss later). Your investors will only have a cursory interest, if any, in who your director will be. Your investors are business people. They've likely made you fully responsible for the entire production, including the hiring and firing. Just as long as *you bring in the movie on time, on budget*. Studio bosses at the major companies hire the Big Guys, leading directors, to direct their leading movies and a leading producer and a leading cast. Except in the rarest of situations when one of the leading people is so leading as to be a super lead or a super-super lead, the studio maintains creative control over each leading person by enforcing that provision in his or her contract.

If you want to get your low-budget movie completed and looking good enough to be a major-company film, you must maintain both administrative and creative control of your film. Don't let the director or one of his or her assistants get away with dismissing your questions by telling you that you wouldn't understand the problem. Instead, ask the person to give you the benefit of the doubt and explain the problem to you, so that you may contribute to its resolution, thereby keeping the show moving and calming all those inner turmoils that many talented directors, their staffs, and actors seem so movably clenched about. Your job is to disentangle their difficulties. Strange, how often their problems are blown out of proportion, so solvable if they'd only share them with others who are trained to handle administrative and management situations. Some creative people seem to naturally back off from advice from accountants, business people, bankers, lawyers, and administrators. Producers assume the risk of keeping talent on the track, huffing and puffing, if necessary, but on the track to their destination: Getting the movie done.

Your efforts toward insisting that the director, subordinates, and actors are making *your* movie will probably be unending. They'll likely want to make *their* movie. Don't buckle under. Inquire about the reputations of those directors you are considering. One method of investigation, often illuminating, is to ask the director for six references, three from friends and three from enemies. Phone all of them to form a picture of your potential director's capabilities and character. Maybe the director's enemies are bad guys themselves, the kind of people you wouldn't like either. What you're seeking is a consensus as to how the director is to work with in real situations, in the heat of battle, during the filming of a movie. A company of people making a movie is as much or even more militaristic than the military. Your director is a high-ranking officer in the line of command. Spend time with him or her prior to hiring, prior to placing the director on the line as your creative leader.

Now, what to pay the director? An equitable figure is $35,800 plus 1½ percent of the profits of the movie, if any. During preproduction, the producer's staff is shared by the director. During and after production, there is plenty of help, as you will see later in Part 2.

Lead Actors

The stars of your movie are the actors with the leading roles—let's assume there are three. Let's also assume that this will be a four-week shoot, six days a week, at least twelve and maybe fifteen to eighteen hours of work each day. You will want your actors on location during those four weeks, plus one or two weeks before the shoot, for rehearsals. That's five or six weeks' time, whether or not they're in front of the camera every day. You'll want them with you on location so that nothing or almost nothing happens to them physically. Remember, the actual time span of your film may be only a day or two or three. You'll want your actors to maintain their opening-day appearances all during the four weeks! That means little, if any, variance in weight and coloring. If actors go out one weekend and get sunburned, you're in trouble, especially with the makeup department. Do your best to keep them healthy and try to dissuade them from intoxicating themselves or taking unnecessary risks on Sundays. You may find that an actor who complains about walking 10 feet for fifteen takes on Friday may go out on a 10-mile hike on a dusty road on Sunday, "to get rid of tensions," and returns with swollen, bleeding feet. You'll learn that what seems rational to you may be considered suppression of individual freedom by talent. Get used to it. Deal with it as best you can.

You'll want to get as much star power as you possibly can in your leads. Enough, at least, to encourage an eventual network television sale, following theatrical distribution. *A network sale may very well return enough money to cover the full cost of your production.* Having stars who are recognizable names, who carry some *box-office appeal,* is highly recommended. It is like carrying insurance, which, while not guaranteed, does offer you a measure of eventual prosperity through a possible television sale. The fact that you're making a movie intended to compete with other movies in the commercial marketplace should be apparent. As a first-timer, you must over and over again convince yourself and others that you're not making a "home" movie.

Star One receives $20,000; Star Two receives $15,000; Star Three receives $12,500. Total: $47,500.

Supporting Actors
The salary range for supporting, bit, and feature actors will vary from $150 per day to $750 per six-day week (they work the sixth day gratis). Let's assume you need forty supporting actors and each actor has at least one line of dialogue (speaking parts cost more). What will it all cost? Hard to estimate, but as a working guide, let's decide on $22,200.

Extras
All those spectators for the crowd scenes are usually amateurs. It usually takes between three and six hours of straight work to get one minute of screentime. That's the rule of thumb for independent productions. For example, if you want to complete

the photography for your ninety-minute movie in twenty-four days (six days a week for four weeks), you'll have to get almost four minutes of screentime each day. That's about double the screentime that the major companies get. But you're an independent working under the gun, on the run to do your thing faster and more economically. Your extras will be selected from the general population around your shooting location. They don't have the experience to know that their services may be needed over a three- or even six-hour period, or longer. Tell them about the time requirements before they sign up. Tell them it doesn't take one minute to shoot a one-minute scene—that there may be five or ten or fifteen takes for each shot before the director is satisfied. You don't want to be in the position of filming a dozen extras who have a clear physical appearance on the screen and then find out that six of them had to go back to school or home for dinner. That sort of thing leaves you high and dry and without continuity on the screen. Spend some extra time with the extras and let them know they're in for the same work with the same standards of conduct and time requirements as anyone else in the shoot.

    If push comes to shove and you can't find any extras, look behind the cameras and ask for volunteers from among the crew. Tell them anything; tell them you're going to make each of them "a star."

Let's figure 200 extras at a cost of $6,320.

SUMMARY OF
ABOVE-THE-LINE EXPENSES

Story and screenplay	$12,400
Producer and staff	52,200
Associate producer and staff	16,400
Director	35,800
Lead actors	47,500
Supporting actors	22,200
Extras	6,320
Above-the-line sub-total	$192,820

CHAPTER 6

BELOW-THE-LINE COSTS

Below-the-line costs are almost always in flux. You've got to pay strict attention to these costs *daily* to keep them in line with your cost and efficiency projections. Just how to do this will be discussed later in Part 2. For now, let's examine below-the-line costs in the order in which they usually appear: production staff, set operation, laboratories, sound, music, location, tests and publicity, insurance and taxes, legal and overhead, and miscellaneous.

PRODUCTION STAFF

The Production Manager
The production manager (PM) is the person who runs the entire company on location. His or her job ends after the principal photography is completed; the manager of production isn't involved in postproduction matters.

Secure the full-time services of a production manager right from the start. The PM should be in on most, if not all, meetings having to do with the preproduction planning and principal photography. Part of a good production manager's job is reviewing the script. You'll want the PM's input. Especially so for three areas of prime importance when you are still in the concept stage of the film's development. You'll want the PM's judgments on the *workability* of the script. The questions he or she must address are difficult. In examining the script the PM has to advise you whether, and why, shots and scenes and sequences will in fact work—be producible in the film medium—or not work.

The PM should have the capacity to conceptualize scenes, perhaps render some drawings, and tell you just what you'll need in terms of manpower and material to accomplish the task of transferring script to film. Second, the PM must advise you on the *probable costs*, by the script page, of converting the script into the movie you desire. Third, you'll need the PM's advice on how much *time* it will take, by the page, to make your movie. Time and money will be the probable top two enemies for you all the way through filming. Knowing what your needs are prior to shooting the movie, structuring a production that has a good chance of working according to schedule, preparing detailed answers to detailed questions, can and will go a long way toward eventual success. Later on in Part 2 you will structure a two-day production sheet.

Your production manager is likely to be the most knowledgeable person in the entire production company. The PM should know how to make a movie. If not, you're dead from the start. Just as the director is charged with responsibility for getting what you want on the screen, your production manager is charged with getting people and machinery and material to work properly—on time and within budget. The production manager is the one person through whom the producer talks and sees. The production manager even holds the producers accountable for their work and actions. The PM pays all the bills, salaries, and expenses and demands reasons and vouchers for all expenditures. The PM, man or woman, is the "bad guy" on location, the one who asks the hard questions, makes the demands and keeps everyone going about their jobs without wasted effort or extra spending on items he or she judges the movie can be made without.

One of the ways the production manager *controls* a movie is with the aid of a production report for each day's work.

Generally it will describe what each of the following persons was assigned to do that day and just what they actually did. Work assignments and crew size will vary from movie to movie; this is simply a guide. It will, of course, introduce you to a sample staff:

Director
Director of photography
Camera person
Assistant production manager
Assistant director
Art and set director
Assistant art and set director
Chief, set construction
Carpenter
Hair dresser
Special-effects person
Special-effects assistant
Stunt person
Sound operator
Assistant sound operator
Electrician
Assistant electrician
Grips (4)
Wardrobe
Property master
Props
Assistant props
Makeup
Painter (if any)
First-aid person (if any)
Unit publicist
Production assistants (2)
Script person
Laborers (if any)
Wranglers (if any)
Generator operator (if any)
Technical advisers (if any)

The PM will note just what each member of the staff accomplished during the daily shoot and comment on their health and behavior that day. Why health and behavior? Because a copy of the report is sent to the insurance company. Your insurer wants to know about illnesses, malingering, or any manifestation of unusual behavior. So do you, because if there are any delays because of human error or sickness, you'll want to have an official record for any possible insurance claim. Through a recitation of the facts, the production report should read like a businesslike record of the daily progress your movie is making. This daily report, usually signed by the PM and assistant director (AD), is a profile of the work attempted and accomplished by your company on the location shoot.

In addition to the above, there is a listing of all major equipment, for example, cameras, cars, buses, trucks, and generators. You'll get the hang of it; if you can see it, list it! Don't forget those specialists who work on set operations, such as public-address operators and local labor. The report should also describe the following items:

The set(s) worked on

The set number(s) and location(s)

What time everyone awakened

What everyone had for breakfast, lunch, dinner, and snacks; when they were fed

What time the production got started

What time everyone wrapped (quit) for the day

What number scenes on what script pages were shot that day

How many scenes were shot previously during production

List of setups (a camera position and lighting arrangement), minutes, seconds, retakes, photographed stills, added scenes, dialogue changes, sound and soundtracks done that day and prior to that day

List of exact picture negative footage used that day and cumulatively; ditto for soundtrack negative

List of each member of the cast, when they began their workday, the amount of time they spent on the sets and how many hours they worked, together with the number of hours they worked since the shoot began

List of minutes, pages, number of takes, number of takes per setup. The camera crew and sound crew make up separate reports of their daily activity. The camera crew notes all the daily scene numbers shot, take numbers, amount of footage, and whether it was shot with sound or without sound. In addition, the report, which goes with the film to the processing lab, carries instructions as to which takes should be printed to make the dailies and which should just have the negative developed but not processed into positive print. The sound report usually carries the scene numbers, whether or not the sound equalization is high or low, whether a filter was used to record the sound, the speed the sound was recorded at, and any special remarks or instructions the sound person believes will help the lab, so that when the sound is transferred to film it will sound the way the director intended it to sound.

Summary of twenty-five to thirty-five words of the plans for the next day's shoot, which serves as a working tool in helping everyone define upcoming goals.

By now you're beginning to realize that the production manager does more work than anyone. In fact, the PM's usually busy filling out forms into the early morning. Make sure the PM you hire has stamina. The PM's likely to be the first one up, usually at 5:30 a.m., and the last to go to sleep, around 2:30 a.m., *everyday for four weeks!* Sundays? The PM will probably only work eight hours, a short-short day, getting files together and briefing the producer and director.

The PM also makes up a Daily Production Schedule or Call Sheet. It is hung outside the production office for everyone to see and contains the following information: The shots and scenes that are to be done that day, what page of the script they're on, what time everything will take place, at what location(s), what might be needed for special effects, props, and property to accomplish certain action, and at what time the needed members of the cast must be on location. Actors do sometimes like to look at the Call Sheet and find they've got a day off! The Call Sheet will also list wardrobe and makeup and hairdressing needed for each cast member who is performing that day. A copy of the Call Sheet is attached to the daily production report at the end of each day's shooting.

The PM's office also makes up a Location Form for each day's shoot, which includes the following: script pages, scenes, day or night shooting, action, cast, wardrobe, setups (camera placements), crew members, material, and machinery.

You'll want everything to function properly and smoothly. The posting of the Location Form and its distribution to all crew members allows them to know what's happening each and every day. As the shoot progresses, peer pressure among the crew increases. Everyone begins to realize that "interdependence" is a productive way of life, the only way the movie will be completed as a quality work of art and be brought in on time and budget.

Planning helps. In the long run it saves time and, because you and others have thought about and discussed production problems and objectives, you'll all feel personally involved. It means hard work but it's worth it on many levels, not the least important being the good feeling that comes from fully informed artists, artisans, and craftspeople working together as a team.

The PM also distributes release forms, which give you permission to photograph persons and places and show the photo commercially. Make sure you get them signed! You don't want people saying they never signed one after the movie is made and shown. Once again, advance planning helps avert a potential disaster, like a lawsuit from cast members who claim you never got permission to photograph them for your movie. There are people in this world who may balk for no reason when they see themselves on a screen. Or, they may just not like the way the movie turned out. Don't risk a losing lawsuit by failing to provide releases for extras as well as for property, such as interiors and exteriors of homes you plan to use in the movie. In this instance, secure the written approval of the homeowner in advance.

What are you going to pay your production manager? I suggest $21,600 plus ½ of 1 percent of profits, if any. I think you'll agree the PM's worth it.

BALANCE OF YOUR
PRODUCTION STAFF

Continuity/Script Person

A continuity person keeps track of what's happening. She or he works closely with the director all during the shoot. The continuity person on an independent movie is sometimes referred to as the script clerk or script person.

The scenes in your script will be shot out of order, out of context. For example, suppose Location A, Set A appears on pages 6, 16, 56, and 86. Because it is economical—time to construct and decorate that set, time and manpower to get there—you will shoot pages 6, 16, 56, and 86 back to back. Then you can "strike" the set—tear it down because you are finished with it—and move the cameras and lights and personnel to another set. The trick is to get your actors scheduled the same way. For example, if a bit player is scheduled for a Wednesday shoot and another shoot the following Monday, you would have to pay the actor for one week's work. In this case, you would try to schedule the bit player for two consecutive days and pay him or her for just two days of work. The sensible scheduling of actors pays dividends by cutting down on payroll.

The script person must be fully aware of the need to make scenes connect, to make sure that the actor wearing a gold ring on page 16 is also wearing it on page 56—and, possibly because of the storyline is not wearing it on pages 6 and 86.

The script person takes a Polaroid still every time a shot ends. When the director calls out "cut" to the camera operator and "freeze" to the actors, the photograph is snapped, so that when the next "take" is made the actors will be placed in their proper positions. The instant photo must be of the highest quality to give a good facsimile of what the shot will look like on the screen. So you'll need a rather expensive camera and quality film to do the job.

The script person also maintains a journal of total segment time for each day's shooting. For example, suppose you have fifteen setups for one scene, covering 75 takes. The script person will list each take and each "print." There may be four takes, but the director may decide to print only two. After viewing the dailies, you can decide which of the two to keep for editing. The script person describes each shot in terms of action and material and actors. If a take is no good, the script person records the director's evaluation as to why it didn't work. For example, a shot may be close-up on Joe or on Jessie's dance or it may be an opening dolly shot—a camera and camera operator mounted on railroad-type tracks, and a dolly, so that the camera can be pushed smoothly around a room for a traveling shot. The script person notes the exact time in minutes and seconds for each shot. You may have worked twelve hours but filmed for only forty-five minutes, ending up with three or four minutes of screentime.

Forty-five minutes of filming requires 3,350 feet of 35 mm negative. To get your ninety-minute movie, you may shoot between 60,000 and 120,000 feet of film; at around 20 cents a foot, that's $12,000 to $24,000. You are likely to use about 100,000 feet, shooting at a 12 to 1 ratio—amount of footage shot as against amount of footage used (ninety minutes equals 8,100 feet). A word of caution: Because film costs are in large part dependent upon the petroleum industry, film stock prices are likely to increase in the future.

What will you pay the script person for his or her services? Make it $2,000 for four weeks.

If you want the script person to function up to maximum capacity, hire an assistant script person to transcribe all the data, type it, and double-check everything every day with the script person. Pay $1,250.

Production and Direction Assistants

Your assistant production manager should be an accountant, a master bookkeeper, or have a master's degree in business administration. This person is almost exclusively involved with paper work, numbers, reports, forms, and proper record-keeping. Pay this person $6,330 in our hypothetical budget.

Your first assistant director (AD) is likely to be the director's liaison with the producers and the production manager. Both the first assistant production manager and first assistant director help the director to conceptualize shots and scenes. One of them should be an artist who can render drawings of the way shots will work—where the cameras and lighting will be, where the actors will be, how they will move in a set location. An AD's sketch resembles those chalked blackboard game plans of football coaches, full of X's and O's and dots and dashes and broken lines and arrows. For movement and action, these pictorial representations of shots are invaluable. Don't make a movie without them. Pay the first assistant director $6,500 and the first assistant production manager, $3,150. They'll just have to bask in the glory of their titles. That's the way it is in many movie jobs—either money or glory, usually, glory.

The director works closely with the two assistants, and you can be sure that they will be very loyal. After all, they want the screen credit and the experience of working with a director because they, too, want to be full-fledged directors one day. They list scene numbers, shot numbers, script pages, direction (action), dialogue, and describe screen direction (blocking) for each scene, draw camera action and define the lighting needs, effects, and sound. They'll do it all. It's their job. In addition, the first AD rehearses talent when the director is jammed with other tasks. It's also likely that the first assistant director is responsible for the screaming on the set. He or she screams for everyone on the set to quiet down. By assuming this somewhat noisy but necessary responsibility, the AD, in effect, spares the director from performing the constant ritual of calling for law and order on the set.

The reality is that you've got about thirty-five crew members doing their jobs; there is lots of equipment everywhere and people are trying to make a place for themselves. The director has rehearsed the actors for content, but the assistant director usually directs action. The AD tells the actors and camera operator just where and when the action of the scene starts and ends. To put it plainly, the director tells the actors what to do, but the first AD frames the shot physically. Meanwhile, the first assistant production manager may be on the next set, at the next location, checking and double-checking that everything is the way the director wants it. Three things are usually going on at once: (1) planning upcoming scenes, (2) doing the scenes, and (3) planning for the next scene (illustrated later in Part 2).

Everytime one task ends, another task begins. It's a continuing process, an evolving continuity—of planning-doing-planning without end, except, of course, for the last shot of the last scene when the director calls out "this is a wrap";—sweet words to a crew on a long shoot, such as a feature movie. "Wrap" means the end, period—but only for those involved in the principal photography. It's just the beginning for those who will be working on the movie during postproduction.

Secretary

Along with the associate producer, director, first assistant director, and the art director, a secretary, assigned to the production manager's office, should be working during the preproduction period. A film requires tons of office work—forms, requests, typing, and photocopying of material. A secretary also disseminates information among the crew and cast. Figure the secretary's salary at $3,450.

Production Clerks

Two production clerks, one to handle transportation exclusively and the other to provide for all the other details will be required. The transportation clerk arranges the arrivals and departures of the cast, the arrivals and departures of the crew, and secures all the vehicles needed in the movie, either as props or working vehicles.

Personnel arrive by automobile, plane, train, bus, truck and motorcycle. The transportation clerk will plan for and provide all modes of travel. Special attention to scheduling and weather are, of course, factors to deal with. The transportation clerk will have on file a massive accumulation of timetables and travel contingencies.

In addition, the cast and crew must be transported from their arrival point to the company location. The clerk sends out drivers to pick up people and their luggage at many different terminals. This person's job ends only after every member of the company has left for home.

The other production clerk attends to every other detail necessary to maintain a smooth flow of company matters. He or she is on the phone or on the run, constantly. Both production clerks are charged with providing an orderly, efficient, and uneventful scheduling of production-office needs, which can also include the purchase and distribution of champagne, on orders from the producer, to townspeople who have been pleasant and cooperative. Pay the clerk in charge of transportation $1,750 and the clerk in charge of general details, who will be needed during postproduction as well, say, $3,450.

Advisers, Casting Director and Staff

The next item in the production staff category covers elective expenses. But like most electives, they become necessities. If you have fight scenes, dueling scenes, dance scenes, a choreographer is a necessity. Many actors can't ride horses or swim or jump or throw a football. Instructors can teach them how to do it and how to do it authentically. For these coaches or technical advisers, add another $9,800. If the results of their labor are not evident when you see the rushes, fire them and hire other professionals. Part of your job is to assess their work and to make decisions you can live with.

Because your first film will be a very personal adventure, for you and your associates, the selection of actors for the film should be a joint responsibility of the producer, the associate producer and director. Interview everyone who applies to work on the production, not only those who will serve behind the camera, but also those who will perform in front of it. Hold open auditions. To encourage a large turnout, place a small ad in the newspaper and send out a press release to a local columnist. Word will travel fast among area actors, even regional ones. They'll be there. Hordes of applicants will reply, all with stars in their eyes. From dinner theaters, local theaters, neighborhood theaters, colleges, drama schools, art schools, regional playhouses, even faraway places.

Give them a scripted page to read, perhaps something from the part they are trying out for. If they do well, call them back. If they do well again, give them a brief screen test, inexpensively, on 16mm film. Have them act and interact with other prospective cast members. You'll begin to notice many things about the auditioners. People look differently on film than they do in person. There is something about film that brings out certain personal qualities. You'll be searching for "screen presence," a certain box-office quality, star power. It's really very subjective, and to top it all, you must live with your choices for the full length of the movie. You'll be judging their acting ability, the way they carry themselves alone and with someone else. Great attention should be paid to eyes. My own feeling is that movie acting is about 75 percent eye and facial movement. So many shots are close-ups (CU) or extreme close-ups (ECU); also sometimes called very close-ups, (VCU). Close-ups convey the *feeling* in a motion picture. The exaggerated eye, facial, and body movements characteristic of stage acting won't do on film. It's a subtler medium. The film actor is larger than life on the screen; the stage performer is either life size or a diminishing figure, playing to the last row in the balcony.

After you have screened the tests, you may still be undecided about casting one or more actors. Go back to Go. Start the whole process over again. You must make your own decisions about acting talent. The process of selection will force you and your associates to start making decisions, to assume the responsibility for your actions as individuals and executives. It will bring you closer together as a team, a small team, each aware of the other's strengths and weaknesses. Not belaboring them, but, instead, taking up the slack, filling in for each other's deficiencies and respecting each other's strengths. Your joint decision will preclude any Monday morning quarterbacking— blame for a bad decision and praise for a good one will be shared equally.

The total cost so far for the production staff is $59,280. It sure adds up quickly.

Director of Photography and Staff
The director of photography (DP) on a low-to-medium-budget movie is the leading technician/crafts person of the film. The DP heads the camera department and directs the lighting and grip (all equipment other than camera or sound) departments. Following a series of discussions with the producer and director, the DP draws up an equipment list, scouts locations, and makes plans about filming requirements, including equipment, personnel, and the time necessary to complete these tasks. The DP and the production manager coordinate the technical aspects of the production.

Because of the irregular nature of film production, your equipment rental house should be kept advised months in advance of production plans so that cameras and other equipment will be available when you need them. The DP decides on all lenses, including zoom and high-speed lenses, and camera accessories, including film magazines, batteries, accessory cables, and filters. If you are filming in extreme heat or cold or wet or humid weather, or even very dirty situations such as wind-blown sand or mud, you may require special preparation work for your equipment from the rental house.

The script will suggest various combinations of camera mountings: for static shots, a tripod of a suitable height; for camera movement, a dolly (movable platform), crane (platform giving vertical movement), or special mountings for hand-held use or attachment to a moving vehicle such as a car, bus, or helicopter. For roving-eye-type shots, the DP may prefer a Steady-Cam, which provides greater than usual flexibility when other mountings are impractical, for example, when the subject and camera are moving on stairs where it is difficult to build a proper camera support or where the area is so small that the camera support roadway would be in the shot. A Steady-Cam, which works in conjunction with a TV monitor, allows the scene you are shooting to be seen simultaneously on the monitor. It's a wonderfully helpful device for all filmmakers.

In discussions with the gaffer (chief electrician), the DP will plan the lighting needs of the production. The DP will often order all required lights, stands, and accessories through the production manager. The DP then reviews with the key grip (chief grip) the grip equipment needs; for example, flags, gels, diffusions, and nets and silks, which are used to modify and control light. The DP will also discuss with the key grip certain foreseeable problems in camera movement or hand-rigging; for example, very high placement of equipment, unusual angles, and the rigging of extra large (larger than 20- by 20-feet square) flags and silks.

Moving from the planning stage to the principal photography itself, the DP's duties include choice of camera angle, composition (esthetically effective framing of a shot), continuity (placement of the camera), and photographic effect (the "look" of the shot). The director calls for action only when the DP advises that lighting and camera are ready. The DP is also concerned with and responsible for equipment and personnel.

In our hypothetical budget, the DP's staff includes a first assistant camera operator, who is paid $2,800. He or she is responsible for the readiness of the camera so that the DP can walk up to the camera, look into the eyepiece and shoot, and make focus changes or focal-length changes (i.e., zoom) during filming.

The second assistant camera operator, who helps in these duties, is paid $2,000. The second assistant and the loader, who is paid $1,600, are responsible for loading and unloading the film magazines, maintaining camera reports for each roll of film, operating the slate (clapboard used for identifying each "take"), packing the film for shipment to the lab, and assisting in any other manner, as needed. Assuming your script will call for some second-unit (second-camera-group) work, figure another $2,200.

To fulfill your contractual obligations to the eventual distributor, you will usually have to supply 100 to 150 still photographs of all significant action scenes as well as portraits of your major stars for publicity purposes, such as newspaper reproduction. Figure $1,000 for the still photographs.

The DP, who will be working during preproduction as well as principal photography, is your highest paid technician: $14,000.

Electrical Department
The electrical department is headed by the gaffer (electrician), whose primary responsibility is to provide all the electrical needs for each and every shot in the movie, as required by the DP's lighting plan. Every time the camera position is changed, every time there is another setup, a lighting change is usually also necessary.

The gaffer supervises not only the placement of lighting fixtures but also the control of the amount of light from those fixtures as they illuminate the set through the use of barn doors (hinged, solid black doors attached to the front of the light), scrims (a metal mesh that fits in front of the light to control intensity), and possibly flood-spot adjustments for the spotlights. In addition to spotlights, the gaffer may use softlights (indirect lighting fixtures).

The gaffer is also responsible for maintaining sufficient electrical current through the use of either existing electrical service or a generator and planning the distribution of the electricity through cables to the various fixtures. If you are filming in an ordinary house, including single 5,000- and 10,000-watt bulbs, you won't be able to plug your lights into the wall. Instead, the gaffer will tie directly into the power cable at the fuse box, which is usually in the basement. From the fuse box, the gaffer will normally prepare a run of three or four large cables to the set.

The gaffer, who is paid $3,500, supervises the work of three assistants: Best Boy, who is the first assistant gaffer, $2,450, and two other assistants at $1,650 each. Except for film stunts, electricity is potentially the source of greatest danger in your production. Your electricians must be sober, mature, experienced, and intelligent. For your own peace of mind, and the insurance company's, hire professionals only!

A tip about temperature in regard to color film: Your film will probably be balanced for 3,200 degrees Kelvin, which is also the color temperature of the lights. If you mix your tungsten lighting, daylight (5,000-plus degrees Kelvin), and/or fluorescent lighting, you will need to filter either the camera or the lighting in order to maintain true colors on the film. In other words, daylight without filtering the camera will register much too blue on film. Fluorescent lighting will register as ugly green. These problems can be overcome through the proper use of various filters.

Grips

The key grip supervises the operation of all grip equipment— flags, nets (cloth mesh for screening light), silks (white cloths for modifying light), parallels (scaffolding), rigging (rope, pipe, lumber, or anything that's available), camera dolly, and dolly track—during the shoot. Grips are also responsible for the movement of camera dollies as well as other equipment. They provide the "muscle." The key grip gets $2,700; the first assistant, $1,800, and two additional set-operation grips, $1,550 each.

Sound

The sound person and his or her assistant, a boom operator, are responsible for recording all the sound required for the film—dialogue, ambience, and effects—that can be obtained on location. The sound chief operates the tape recorder, most likely a Nagra with ¼-inch tape, and the boom operator places the microphones in position for recording optimum sound. Microphone placement is the most important variable to be considered in recording good sound. The sound chief must be experienced and knowledgeable about the characteristics of all types of microphones as well as the situations likely to be encountered during production. A constant problem, for example, is the positioning of the mike to record the type of sound required and at the same time keeping it hidden from the camera and unaffected by extraneous noise or noisemakers. If it isn't feasible to secure because of location noise, "scratch" (noisy) sound is recorded as an aid for dubbing in clear sound at a later time.

Communication between the sound department and other departments is essential. Static electricity, for example, caused by synthetic clothing, will be picked up as static noise on the sound track. Consequently, the wardrobe department should be advised to dress the characters in cotton (including undergarments).

The sound chief is also required to fill out a sound report describing the sound effect recorded and identifying the scene for which it is required (illustrated later in Part 2) which is sent with the tape to the transfer house.

The sound chief: $3,000; the boom operator: $1200.

Art Director

The art director is primarily responsible for the *things* that are filmed—the clothing, makeup, and hairdressing of the actors. Directly responsible to the director, the art director is involved during the preproduction stage through the end of principal photography. During preproduction, he or she attends all conferences with the producer and director dealing with the "look" of the movie. He or she should be knowledgeable about the settings—for example, bars, planes, classrooms, or gyms and should know, from first-hand experience, just what the particular setting is really like so that a sense of contemporary realism or period authenticity can be captured realistically on film. The art director should seek "perfection" in the look of the movie, but within budget. The art director usually has a tendency to spend and spend to get things "just right." You've got to stand firm to keep him or her from going overboard—over budget. The art director, who supervises a large staff: $9,200. The assistant art director: $4,200.

The set supervisor who is responsible for carrying out the designs of the art director, dressing all the sets and in a studio situation would be responsible for having the set built: $3,500.

Property Personnel, Set Dressers, and Support Labor

A property chief ($4,200) and an assistant ($3,500) are responsible for acquiring, caring for, and returning all properties used during production and insuring that all hand props (cigarettes, rings, umbrellas) are available to the cast. A chief set dresser ($3,600) and an assistant ($3,000) are responsible for preparing sets at each location for filming. For extra labor to assist in the preparation and striking of particularly difficult sets: $2,600. Carpenters, painters, and other skilled workers—you may need breakaway shelves and chairs, even breakaway buildings: $10,800. Total: $27,700.

Wardrobe

The wardrobe chief ($3,000), who is responsible for acquiring, perhaps designing, wardrobe for the cast, is assisted by second wardrobe ($2,400) and third ($900). They maintain and protect all wardrobe, including cleaning and sewing, and also dress the cast in the proper costumes for each scene. For a seamstress and extra help for alterations and fittings: $250.

Makeup

Key makeup ($4,800), who is responsible for designing all makeup, is assisted by second makeup ($1800), a hairdresser ($2,400) and an assistant hairdresser ($1,000). This group must keep in mind that each cast member is likely to need a different type of makeup and that different scenes may require makeup changes. They must also maintain sufficient makeup supplies and other necessary equipment.

Special Effects

The special-effects chief ($3,200) and assistant ($1,500) are in charge of designing, preparing, and executing all special effects.

Special effects, in the motion-picture industry, include all things that do not happen naturally and/or all things that an average actor cannot normally or easily accomplish. These technicians help to convert fantasy into reality, on cue.

Security
To protect the sets from strangers, you'll need the services of two security officers: $2,100.

Total Cost Production Staff: $171,980

SET OPERATION

Camera:	Equipment rentals, $6,900; purchases, $1,000.
Electrical:	Equipment rentals, $9,500; purchases, $3,500; power, $1,500.
Grip:	Equipment rentals, $6,000; purchases, $500.
Sound:	Equipment rentals, $2,000; purchases, $900.
Art:	Equipment rentals, $10,400; purchases, $22,400.

Total Cost Set Operation: $64,600

FILM

Raw Stock Purchases
For your 8,100-foot, ninety-minute movie, buy 100,000 feet of raw stock (film negative): $20,000 (20 cents a foot, subject to price changes, of course).

Why 100,000 feet? Because, first, you will lose 2,000 to 3,000 feet in unavoidable waste when loading the camera and checking for scratches. You will probably waste another 10,000 feet just between the time the director calls for the camera to roll until the actors actually start performing and from the time when the actors stop performing and the camera finally stops rolling. Now, you are down to 87,000 to 88,000 feet of film. You will also have "short ends," a minute's worth of film left in the magazine when you have a three-minute scene to shoot. You will remove the short end and store it, intending to use it for a forty-five second scene later in the shoot. But you may never have a future occasion to use it, or you may lose confidence in its stability once it has been removed from its original moistureproof container. Short ends could add to up another 10,000 feet of lost film during the course of your production. (Short ends can be sold for scrap or be used in still photography. Less fortunate producers willing to gamble with their "gold," another term for raw stock, because they have to, will buy it.) We are now down to 77,000 or 78,000 feet of film. Inexperienced filmmakers who do not take this waste into consideration are like navigators who do not realize just how far the fuel supply will go. You may never make it to the end of your film.

Of the remaining 77,000 or 78,000 feet, 35,000 to 45,000 feet will be printed to work with during the editing process. From that footage, you will eventually select about 8,100 feet for your ninety-minute movie.

Laboratories

The film lab will develop your negative for approximately $7,500 and make a work print for about $5,500. The transfer of sound from 1/4-inch tape to 35mm sprocketed magnetic tape will cost $2,000 plus $1,000 in materials. Other lab expenses include magnetic sound track for your music score and dubbing: $1,000. Internegatives, composite print and answer print: $12,000.

An internegative, also called a CRI (color reversal internegative), is a negative made from your original negative and is used to make your positive prints. This will lessen the chance of any damage to your original negative, your gold. The composite print is the first print that includes both your picture and optical sound track on one piece of film. An answer print is just that. Sit back, look at it very carefully. It's your movie. The one you intend to sell to a distributor and have exhibited in theaters around the world.

Other item costs, opticals (fades, dissolves, wipes), reprints, titles (opening and closing), coating (on the work prints), represent a combined $11,250.

Projection fees, shipment of dailies, reels and leader, and process plates may total $3,700 in your hypothetical budget.

POST PRODUCTION

Editing

Your editorial staff will include a supervising editor, an assistant cutter, a second assistant editor, and a negative cutter.

To arrange all the printed footage into a whole movie, the editors begin by synchronizing the transferred sound with the picture. Then they break down all the reels of processed film into individual scenes, thereby collecting all similar and connecting visuals, the process of assembling the movie by its various parts. Once everything is collated and labeled, a "rough cut" of your entire movie, from beginning to end, is constructed. A rough assembly of your script in film form, it is considerably longer than your intended final film. The editors try to put in all the likely possibilities with the best footage available. They may try for two or three endings to a given scene, for example, in an effort to judge which one gives the best rhythm, pacing, visual, action, dramatic feeling, mood—the "look and feel" you have been striving for.

It's possible that you will make several rough cuts, each time reducing the running time of the movie, until you are satisfied with the overall results. It might mean putting in a less desirable shot or scene so that another, more important shot or scene will play better—or so the movie will play better as a whole. The sum, the movie, is greater than its parts, and to get what you want holistically, you may have to sacrifice small perfections for total quality.

You are working toward a "fine cut," the ultimate film. The almost never-ending process of selection, rejection, and matching, of deciding what works and what doesn't, is all very subjective. In truth, editing is a creative endeavor. It is a process of really rescripting and redirecting the movie. Moreover, through fades, dissolves, and other opticals, the actor's performance, in effect, can be altered. For example, you may have a medium close-up shot of a particular expression on an actor's face, but to light up the scene or to give it dramatic impact, you need a close-up. You can enlarge the frames to get a close-up or extreme close-up to use in the fine cut of the print. You have, in effect, altered the script, direction, lighting, camera, and acting in the take as shot on location.

In view of the obvious need for the editor to know what is intended, what kind of a movie is planned for, and what the director wanted when the take was shot and printed, I recommend that the editor be with you on location. Working closely with the script and/or continuity person, the editor will be fully informed when he or she goes about the job of editing after the shoot. It's good business and, in the long run, can save you considerable time as well. Or you may want to go a step further and instruct the editor to actually synchronize and assemble scenes on location. This work has to be done in any event and by doing it on location, any obviously needed additional footage can be shot while the location facilities and personnel are available. There's little, if any, additional cost to having editing done on location. It can save you the cost of going back a month later and reshooting additional scenes.

Editing costs: chief editor, $10,000; first assistant, $7,500; second assistant, $3,500; negative cutter, $1,400; rent (cutting room), $12,500; supplies and materials, $1,500.

Total Cost Film: $100,350.

MUSIC

What you want to get is music on tape that can be mixed in with the other sound tracks at the final mix. Your composer should be on hand during the rough cut to get an idea of what you are striving for. He or she will write the theme music, music for each character, maybe a song or two. After the music is recorded, the tape will be played while the process of whittling down the rough cut is going on. This time you'll be matching music to visuals.

If you contract for some canned music in the public domain, deal with a reputable concern and make sure that the music you buy hasn't been used for at least twenty years in another film. Get it in writing. Figure music at $7,500. An alternative to a canned music is to produce the music yourself, which means hiring a composer, musicians, singers, renting a studio and instruments, and acquiring all rights. Because considerable planning and scheduling is required for this alternative, it is not something to be undertaken lightly. On a small scale, it can be like the shooting of a movie on location.

Total Cost Music: $7,500.

SOUND

Postproduction sound expenses include the rights to sounds (usually effects) not recorded on location, $2,000, and another

$3,000 for dubbing and looping—labor, material, and space.

The combining of all the sound tracks onto a master track, to be added into your composite print for the final movie, is called mixing. Mixing is usually done by frame, sometimes as closely as two frames at a time (remember, there are twenty-four frames a second), frontwards and backwards, until the various levels of sound are the way you want them. Mixing is a painstaking and costly experience. Budget for ten days, $10,000. One result of your experience: After seeing the film over and over again, frontwards and backwards, you'll likely lose the objectivity to make a critical comment about it.

Total Cost Sound: $15,000.

STUDIOS AND ON-SITE LOCATIONS

Films are produced in studios where the desired environment is created, or on location, where the desired environment already exists.

The major advantage of studio work is that it allows the filmmaker as much control as possible over his or her environment. For example, a studio will offer optimum sound conditions, wild-walls (walls that can be moved, permitting the camera and equipment needed space), and a centralized place to work. A studio will charge for the services and facilities used, such as dressing rooms, kitchens, rest rooms, and offices, as well as the space required. When you rent a studio you rent a large, empty space for a period of time that includes not only the time required for filming but also the time required to build the sets, and strike and remove them from the premises when the shooting is completed. For a living-room set, for example, you would have to build the walls and the floor, furnish it, and restore the premises to their original condition when you're through.

The major drawbacks are the costs involved and scheduling. To cover the large capital expense of running a studio, the studio management is under pressure to keep all spaces booked all the time. If you are running behind schedule or ahead of schedule, you may find that someone else has reserved the time and space you want. Studio rentals can be rigid, especially the busy ones.

Because you want to cut corners, you'll be working with

on-site locations. If you need a living room, secure an existing one that fits your needs and is available from a friend at any time for either no cost or, at most, a small gratuity.

ON-LOCATION MAINTENANCE

The maintenance of the production company on location includes traveling to and from location ($10,000), housing at a hotel or motel and meals at the hotel, on the set, and points between, three well-balanced meals each day plus two or three snacks ($64,000). To cover transportation needs on location (renting station wagons, vans, trucks and covering gas and oil costs), budget $6,000. To rent a location office, arrange for phone service, supplies, and equipment, probably including a duplicating machine, budget $3,500. For gratuities, cash thank-you's for services rendered to the production company, budget $1,500. For scouting the location, budget $3,000. To cover anticipated costs for municipal services and permits, budget $1,000.

Total Cost Location: $89,000.

TEST AND PUBLICITY

Your camera equipment may be shipped to you from the rental house in as many as twenty cases, which may include two cameras, extra film magazines, batteries, cables, lenses, filters, and accessories. The best way to insure that all the components fit together is to set them up and try them out. For example, you don't want to wait until you arrive on location to find out that the motor doesn't fit the camera. To ascertain that your camera is functioning properly and your lenses are sharp, shoot and develop a test film (one day's work by an assistant camera operator and labs). Also included in this cost category are screen tests and makeup tests. Budget $2,000 for preproduction tests and an additional $750 to test special effects during production to see if they really work on film. For advertising, entertainment, publicity stills, and supplies and material, budget $2,500.

Extravagant publicity campaigns cannot be produced for $2,500, but you can at least send out press releases to the major media and try to get your stars on a "talk" show or two.

Total Cost Tests and Publicity: $5,250.

INSURANCE AND TAXES

Some insurance items you can afford, others will be too expensive, and still others you cannot afford to be without. Cast and Key Person insurance, which provides coverage for loss of services by your key people through accident or death, is necessary, and you must budget it as an affordable item. It will cover five or six people—your lead actors, possibly a couple of feature players, and the director. Figure $10,000. Budget an additional $15,000 to cover workman's compensation insurance, public liability insurance and equipment. Add another $3,000 for taxes, licenses, and temporary insurances. Insurance against weather conditions, against loss of or damage to negative film, and against errors and omissions, such as infringement of copyright and invasion of privacy, are not included. Health, welfare, and pension-plan contributions and the employer's share of social-security taxes are not included because the independent contractors who are making your movie are self-employed persons.

Total Cost Insurance and Taxes: $28,000.

Legal and Overhead

Your production company is an association of individuals brought together by contractual duties and obligations. In addition, your company has to comply with municipal, state, and federal statutes. Your attorney will ascertain that you are in compliance with all of them, as well as draw up contracts and assist in settling contractual disputes, if any.

Your attorney's first contractual undertaking will be the proposal for your investors. This is a legal document. And toward the end of production you will need a contract with the distributor, as well as legal advice on its business implications. Your contract with the distributor includes the conditions, if any, under which you'll be paid by the distributor. To arrive at these conditions, both you and the distributor must agree to the definitions of gross gross film rental, gross film rental, net gross film rental, gross net film rental, net film rental, and net net film rental.

You'll be living with these contracts for many years. Make sure they say exactly what you want them to say, and know and understand what you are agreeing to. And make sure that the other party does, too. Budget $20,000 for legal fees.

Overhead includes the expenses of your home office— office suplies, telephone, postage, and accounting. Budget $5,000.

To assure your investors that funds will be available for the movie's completion if the movie goes over budget, secure a $50,000 "completion bond." A completion bond is compensation paid to a bonding company to assure that additional money, a maximum conditional disbursement clearly stated and agreed to, will be released to complete production if it is needed.

Total Cost Legal and Overhead: $75,000.

MISCELLANEOUS

To cover such miscellaneous expenses as coffee and crumpets on the set and sundry unclassified items, such as the cost of this book, budget $500.

Total Cost Miscellaneous: $500.

SUMMARY OF BELOW-THE-LINE EXPENSES

Production staff	$171,980
Set operation	64,600
Laboratories	100,350
Sound	15,000
Music	7,500
Location	89,000
Tests and publicity	5,250
Insurance and taxes	28,000
Legal and overhead	75,000
Miscellaneous	500
	$557,180
Subtotal Above the Line	$192,820
Subtotal Below the Line	557,180
TOTAL BUDGET	$750,000

QUALITY AND COSTS

Beginning filmmakers are always striving for indefinable perfection, a laudatory but dangerous ambition. The beginning tendency is to shoot and shoot take after take to get it just right. This eats up precious time, costs money, taxes the stamina of crew and cast, and ruins your schedule. It's one of the reasons reasonable filmmakers go over budget and behind schedule. It's one thing for an individual to strive for and achieve perfection. It's quite another matter to achieve perfection when thirty people or more are involved together with an acre of machinery, including cameras, lighting, and microphones. You'll have to decide when you've got the best artistic rendition, economically. This is a point of prime importance that you will reflect on continually in your moviemaking career. It is the subject of endless discussions, philosophical conversation, egoistic perceptions, personal values, and artistic interpretations. You'll always be involved in deciding when to end it all and move on to the next thing.

CHAPTER 7

CAUTION: DON'T PROMISE
TO MAKE A MOVIE

Let us assume that neither you nor your friends nor your relatives have the money, singly or in aggregate. And, assume that even if you and/or they did the money wouldn't come from these sources. Your task then is to interest strangers in investing in your movie. How many strangers? What kind of strangers? How do you go about it?

Because there is a legal limit to the number of strangers you can approach for financing, consult your attorney for professional advice right from the start. Generally speaking, if you ask too many people to invest, the Securities and Exchange Commission (SEC) could consider your solicitations to be a public offering and not a private offering. Public offerings, which must be registered with the SEC, must abide by many strict state and federal rules and regulations—a roadblock that can effectively stop you right from the start. Failure to comply with any requirements may squash your entire project, and you may face federal prosecution.

Assuming that you and your attorney have arrived at a suitable number of solicitations and a suitable proposal, a word of severe caution before you make your first offer: that *you cannot, absolutely cannot and must not say* that you are planning to make a movie, that you are going to make a movie that the public will love, a movie that the best distributors and exhibitors will be fighting among themselves to handle, a movie that will do nothing but big business, a movie so unique that the world is waiting with open arms, a movie that will make money, so much money that it will take bank vaults to store the profits. If any of the above doesn't happen, you may be personally liable for your statements, your representations, on which investors relied and therefore invested. Your investors can always come back to you and say you promised them big profits. You can, of course, state that you are making a movie with the intent and hope of making a profit. You cannot promise that the movie will be distributed, or, if distributed, that it will generate a profit.

THE PROPOSAL: FULL DISCLOSURE

Your proposal should be drawn up by you and your attorney, accountant, and business adviser. It will run about twenty-five to fifty pages and may include:

- A brief history of the motion-picture industry
- A more in-depth history of the industry during the previous decade
- A more in-depth history of the independently produced features during the previous decade
- A synopsis of the script
- Résumé of the associate or executive producer
- Résumé of the director
- Résumés of the leading actors
- Why movies do and don't make money
- Why your movie has a chance to make money
- The financial arrangements
- Legal consequences
- Tax considerations and consequences
- Appendix

The proposal will require a considerable amount of research and expertise. *It's a full-disclosure document.* You will be held accountable for every word and thought in it and any promises you make, as well. It must be a *full* disclosure, warts and all. If the movie business is lousy, state it. If you never made a movie before, state it. If your director is new to feature movies, state it. If your lead actor has low blood sugar or a bad back, state it. If your movie has little chance of being distributed or of turning a profit, show it and state it. The proposal must put the potential investor on notice that moviemaking is a very risky business.

A Brief History of the Motion-Picture Industry
This opening section of the proposal should reveal that the principals have a working knowledge of the commercial motion-picture industry. There should be an introductory definition and discussion of industry terms and means so that potential investors may understand the interrelationships between the three pillars of the industry: production, distribution, and exhibition.

A More In-Depth History of the Industry
During the Preceding Decade
The emphasis here is on full discolsure of current industry trends through statistics, which are printed almost weekly in *Variety* as well as in annual statements by the major film companies.

A More In-Depth History of the
Independently Produced Features
During the Preceding Decades
Because your first movie is likely to be independently produced, you must provide a recent history of independently made features: the titles, stories, themes, budgets, box-office grosses, profits and losses. This section, like the others, will require considerable research. You must report the good with the bad, so that your potential investors, relying on your information, can make reasonable, prudent, and judicious decisions on whether to invest or not. To render such a decision, they must be *fully* informed. Your best source of industry statistics is *Variety*.

A Synopsis of the Script
Your synopsis should reflect the tone of your script and include the story, theme, characters, setting, and locations, and some illustrative spoken dialogue. About 1,500 words.

Résumé of the Producer
A complete and truthful disclosure of the producer's movie and business background, the producer's résumé should include both his previous successes and failures.

Résumé of the Associate or Executive Producer
This person, who is likely to be a business person or attorney, may be involved to a greater extent with contracts and legal matters. Here again, full disclosure about his or her past activities in the world of commerce is necessary.

Résumé of the Director
Since this person is generally responsible for the "artistic look" of the movie, the director's ability to complete a movie must be revealed. The investors are once again relying on total disclosure and factual history.

Résumés of the Leading Actors
If contracts with actors have been signed, include their professional backgrounds. Otherwise, define and describe the types of actors you will be seeking. The point is, don't announce someone if he or she isn't already signed.

Why Movies Do and Don't Make Money
Cite statistics, studies, experts. You are delivering the facts as they are, for better or worse. Again, *Variety* is your best bet for industry statistics.

Why Your Movie Has a Chance to Make Money
Relate your intended movie to other existing movies of the same or similar genre. Relate your intended movie to total industry output. Is there a glut or shortage of similar movies? What kinds of movies are going to do well in the near future according to industry predictions? How does your fit in? Is it similar?

Different? Define, describe, compare, and contrast your film with others so that investors may form their own conclusions based on facts.

The Financial Arrangements

Outline the business organization of the project—that is, proprietorship, partnership, or corporation. Generally, independent productions are partnerships, more specifically, limited partnerships. A limited partnership is an association of two or more persons joined together for the purpose of carrying on a business for profit. A limited partnership consists of at least one general partner, who is responsible for the management of the partnership and is *personally* liable for all debts. He or she must also demonstrate financial capability. The limited partners have no say in the management of the partnership and their liability is limited to the extent of their investment in the partnership. The investors are the limited partners. The general partner(s) can be either one of the principals in the project or a corporation. If a corporation is formed for the specific purpose of being the general partner and thus limiting liability, it must have sufficient capital to avoid an IRS ruling that the entire organization be taxed as a corporation. The IRS disregards form and judges content, as does the Securities and Exchange Commission.

All states have statutes specifying the requirements and the form of limited partnership agreements. If you do something wrong because of omission or error, you're still answerable for your actions, however well-intentioned they may be. You must know the legal definition of such terms as "partnership," "general partner," "limited partner," and "fiduciary." You are charged with full understanding of legal language in business dealings, including movies.

You must spell out clearly the nuts and bolts of your organization. For example, cash and/or other securities will flow to the partnership from investors as capital contributions. You must detail how the money will be spent, including escrow accounts until the total capital is raised, organization expenses incurred in getting the business off the ground, and expenditures for the business purposes of the partnership. For example, the purposes of the partnership could be to purchase a completed film from an outside production company, or the partnership itself could be the production company. Or the general partner, as the production company, could sell the film to the partnership.

You will have to detail the source of any revenue generated by the partnership, how expenses will be matched with that revenue in order to determine profit and loss, and how the profit or loss will be distributed to the partners, both general and limited.

You will provide additional details about possible financial contingencies and liabilities, including the safeguarding of funds and assets. This section should spell out all the financial facts so that an investor can have sufficient information on which to base an investment decision.

Legal Consequences
This section must reveal that you are aware of the law and in conformity with the law. Without being fully aware of the law, you can get into serious trouble. There are laws to protect investors—maybe gullible investors at the hands of unscrupulous promoters—as well as laws to which investors must conform. For example, you may want the investor to understand and sign a statement, together with his or her accountant, that he or she has a net worth of perhaps $250,000 and a yearly and stable income of at least $50,000. There are understandings and conditions to be met on both sides. Everyone has to know exactly what he or she is getting into, because there are tremendous risks involved in making any movie. As usually the most risky of movie investments, independent productions require the most disclosure.

The dividing line between a public offering and private offering can be hairy. Among the issues to be considered are: number of shares, number of investors, the financial sophistication of the investors, and whether the offering is to be intrastate or interstate. It is mandatory that you seek the advice of an attorney competent in this area of the law.

Your proposal must be full of *disclaimers*—you must attempt to avoid broken promises and to make sure that everyone knows that the risks are overwhelming and that nothing about your enterprise is guaranteed or even promised. Don't even promise that the sun will rise in the heavens tomorrow.

Tax Considerations and Consequences

You must reveal enough useful information so that an individual investor can interrelate his or her personal tax status with the tax implications of the business entity. You will most likely have a partnership. The partnership as an entity will not pay tax. Instead, items flow through the partnership to the individual partners. It is basically up to the management of the partnership to decide upon the treatment of all business considerations, including tax items. As limited partners, the investors have no right to make management decisions. Therefore, business decisions regarding tax matters must be disclosed in advance so that the investors are fully informed about what they are getting into.

What they are getting into could conceivably be challenged by the IRS after the fact. If you were deficient in your planning and proposal, the IRS could conceivably rule that your partnership is in fact a corporation. This would totally change the tax consequences and/or advantages as promised in your proposal to investors. The IRS could also rule that your partnership does not exist for tax purposes because it is not a business for profit. Or they could call it all a hobby, which would mean that any losses could not be deducted. Your investors have to understand these things. As sophisticated investors, they face possibilities such as these all the time.

There could conceivably be tax benefits available to the investors as a result of their involvement in your project. For example, they may be able to postpone tax liability by deferring the recognition of income. In addition, they can reduce their personal tax liability by their share of the investment tax credit for the year in which the film is completed and put into service for business purposes. No movie, no credit! In addition, the movie has to have a *life* of at least three years for the investor to be entitled to any tax credit. Your movie has to play in the open marketplace.

You, of course, must comply with the tax laws, which are constantly changing, likely as not, not for your benefit.

Appendix

The appendix should include a copy of the limited partnership agreement and a subscription form for purchasing a share in the partnership. It should also include a form for each potential investor to fill out, sign, and have countersigned by his or her accountant, regarding his or her net worth and a permission form, to be signed by the potential investor, giving you the right to investigate his or her credit rating.

CHAPTER 8

THE PROCESS OF PRODUCTION

PREPRODUCTION

Realizing what you have accomplished so far—you have a script and the money to produce the movie—you should begin the preproduction period with great enthusiasm. You should also be very aware of your responsibility to deliver a particular movie on time and on budget, which means, of course, that you must operate within the constraints of deadlines and dollars. The producer, associate producer (you), director, and production manager will meet during the preproduction period to decide on the parameters of your work schedule, using the script and the budget as blueprints for action. You will discuss script analysis, personnel (cast and crew), materials and equipment, and locations within the framework of logistics: when and where you'll be needing what, and how they will get there. You've already done some preliminary work on the script for budgetary purposes. Now you must break down the script, detailing its component parts, listing all those things the script calls for, and deciding how to go about photographing your movie.

Auditioning Actors

Prepare a list of all the characters that will appear in your movie. Start off with the leads, then feature players, bit players, and, finally, extras.

To find your actors, run a few small ads in local newspapers announcing a casting call. Just list the time and place, not the phone number, unless you want to risk getting a thousand calls day and night. Also request a photo (preferably an 8 x 10 black and white glossy) and résumé that can be left with you at the time of the audition. This audition will probably be the first of a series of auditions because of the numbers of people you'll be dealing with. Auditions can be held in a neighborhood theater, the larger the better. At the audition first describe the movie and the characters. Have some sample scripting to be read. Allow each actor a chance to show his or her stuff for a few minutes. You will not only be doing justice to them, but to yourself too, for the thousand or two thousand who audition are potential paying audiences for your movie at, perhaps, $3 or more admission.

Don't count on getting your leads or even your feature actors from these auditions, although you may find one or two. Auditions should produce your bit players and extras, however, and they will be reliable because they are highly motivated.

Actors can also be found by visiting local theaters, including dinner theaters, theater departments at area-wide schools, colleges, and workshops, and contacting casting agents, who may offer to do all the casting for you. If you are interested in certain established actors, call the agents who represent them. You may strike a deal for a lead or a feature player or two.

The overriding consideration for independent producers is accountability. You must be absolutely certain that actors will be available when you need them, that they will show up on time at the right location. You'll want to settle in your head and theirs that each one is a responsible person. Some actors will say they can do anything to get a role. For example, you may ask an actor to prove, in action, what the actor says he or she can do. If a role calls for an actor to swim, and the actor says he or she can, ask the actor to swim and see for yourself. If your actor should sink and nearly drown once the cameras are rolling, it could cost you a bundle.

Check out your actors' health! Moviemaking requires stamina. An actor who breaks out in a rash if looked at cross-eyed is a risk (unless, of course, you need an actor who can break out in a rash on the command of a cross-eyed crew member). If you hire AFTRA (American Federation of Television and Radio Artists) or SAG (Screen Actors Guild) actors you will sign a contract with the union spelling out the rights, duties, and obligations of both parties after negotiating terms with the local business manager of the union.

Except for some additional extras who can be hired on location, all the cast should be hired prior to principal photography. Your director will most likely want to rehearse your leads and feature players several times before actual filming begins.

SETS

Make a list of all required sets, with a description of each one. Then get in your car and go out scouting for them. When you have found them, note their addresses, workability, resources, advantages, and disadvantages. For example, always ask yourself: Is there enough room to set up your behind-the-camera personnel and equipment? Be sure to ask this question of department heads as well before contracting for sets. Then decide on which sets you want, based on their availability, cost and travel requirements.

DRESSING THE ACTORS

Now that you have the actors to play the characters, you need to dress and groom them for their roles. The director and art director define style and fashion giving a visual definition to the movie. Clothing, hairdressing, make-up and accessories are visual dialogue—every bit as important as spoken dialogue. For example, it might be reasonable to give a male farmer a crew-cut but, if your character is a male attorney and you give him crew-cut hair, you are defining the type of person he is or, the type of clients he has.

Once the proper "look" for each character has been determined, then your wardrobe and makeup departments will purchase, fit, catalogue and maintain all clothing. You must make sure that the various costumes needed by the actors are ready before filming. For example, suppose an actor is named John Smith. The script may call for five different wardrobe changes for him. You would have a "John Smith-1" costume, a "John Smith-2" costume, and so forth. Each costume change will be complete from head to toe, in every detail. Now, suppose John Smith's number five wardrobe is to cover a scene that takes place in the rain, or mud or river. You may have several duplicates of all his clothes for these scenes—"John Smith-5A," "John Smith-5B," and so on.

These wardrobe lists are keyed to the script and cross-referenced to make sure that you have provided costumes for every character for every scene.

Similarly, makeup must be designed, purchased, catalogued, stored and ready for use. Special makeup applications, such as those needed for wounds and diseases, must be provided for. Don't underestimate the time requirements and constraints for makeup and, maintaining makeup during rehearsals, meals and a long day's shoot. For example, if an actor wants a Coca-Cola during a break in the shooting, have him or her drink through a straw, so his or her makeup won't be affected.

As for hairdressing, after deciding just what styles are required, you must maintain the proper coiffures for continuity. Remember, your film may be shot over a four-week period, but your story on screen may last only a single day.

To summarize the above items, here are some lists for your use. Use them to dress your actors. Please note how detailed each list is.

Wardrobe
Actor/actress
Character
Costume #
Type of Costume
Effect Desired
Inventory #

Storage

Hat	Gloves	Wardrobe
Scarf	Belt	Continuity
Glasses	Pants	Sequence
Pipe/cigar	Skirt	Previous
Earrings	Socks/stockings	Costume
Tie	Shoes	Next Costume
Shirt/blouse	Overcoat	
Jacket	Muffler	
Jewelry/pins	Underwear (if	
	appropriate)	
Watch	Other:	

Makeup

Actor/actress

Character

Makeup #

Reason for makeup (corrective?)

Effect Desired

Lighting Temperature

Hair	Cheekbones
Temples	Cheek hollows
Forehead	Ears
Brows	Lips
Eyelids	Chin
Eyelashes	Jowls
Under Eyes	Neck
Nose Bridge	Nails
Nose lobes	Hands
Body	Legs
Feet	

Materials:

Base

Highlights

Prosthetics

Special

Liners

Shadows

Pencils

DRESSING THE SET

You have scouted and secured location spaces to match your script needs. Next, the director and art director will detail the specific look they want for each set. Again you'll be making lists of items so that you will be prepared and to provide continuity. For example, suppose we have a table for a banquet scene. You'll need a description of the table or tables. Where will you acquire the table and how will you store it till you are done with it? At which film location will it be used? What story sequence does it relate to? Should it create any particular mood or effect? In what scenes does it appear? Will it be modified, so you can use it in another scene? How will it be moved? How many pieces does it come in and what sizes are they? Who will move it and when? You will also need a floor plan to show the placement of the table on the set. Next, you'll have to deal with the props to be placed on the table—flowers, glasses, plates, utensils, photos. All these props must similarly be acquired, transported, stored, placed where they belong, maintained and used, as required by the script. If there is food, it may have to be prepared and refrigerated. You may need enough quantities for several takes of any given shot. Basically, all you've done is set a banquet table for some event.

In addition to holding all these items, each set must conform to the mood of the scene, whatever that might be. For example, if someone asked you to create a Tod Browning type of mood in a small interior set for a Dracula-horrific look, your notes for dressing the set might read as follows:

Get an Arri 35 mm BL camera with a 1.85 ground glass, a 25-250mm zoom lens, an 85 filter, 2000-watt softlight, a 2000-watt quartz light, two 750-watt solar spots, some spun glass. To get correct effects with eyes, white or yellow contact lenses, or some magenta gel and some half-blue gel.

Get a crystal motor and either 400-feet or 1000-feet rolls. A 400-foot roll delivers about four minutes of film, so for a shooting ratio of ten to one, to get one minute of screentime, we will need three magazines, two batteries, two power cables. For mood, use a number one and number two fog filter, a double filter ring for the zoom, an O'Conner (TM) 100 head, a set of sawed-off Mitchell legs, some spreaders, a show card to reflect light, barn doors (small boxes), stands for all lights, extension cords for 60 amps of electricity, baby tie-ins.

Personnel needed: a set decorator, wardrobe person, hairdresser, makeup person, director, director of photography, script person, sound person, gaffer, grip and all their equipment.

For continuity, keep a photographic record of the table...for day-to-day or, scene-to-scene changes, or perhaps, for a later reshoot. You must do a similar analysis and detail work for anything besides the table that is visible to the camera including, walls and floors. It is the responsibility of your prop person and set dressers to have each set in the movie ready for the camera, crew and cast. They will meet, discuss and plan for each set and keep the director advised of their progress.

SPECIAL EFFECTS

Special effects deals with those things that do not naturally occur. They are artificially caused, on cue, for the camera to record. Examine the script for all special-effects requirements. It is the responsibility of your special-effects person to figure how the effect will be accomplished. After special effects are approved by the director and director of photography as suitable, the special-effects person acquires the materials to carry them out. This may include modifying existing locations and everyday items for a particular purpose. Detailing includes where the effect takes place, what characters will be involved, if a stunt person or double will be required, and who will actually operate and/or cause the effect. Other important considerations include whether or not the effect builds from a previous scene or continues to a following scene. A sense of continuity makes for greater plausibility when the special effect takes place on the screen and the audience accepts the unreal as a reasonable fantasy. The special effect must be an integral part of a scene. For example, a car slipping and sliding down an icy mountain road is likely to skid off the road and crash down the side of the mountain. The carefully orchestrated and filmed crash and ensuing fire are the special effects. This example, as with most special effects, deals with action, *make-believe action, whereby you make the audience believe the effect is reality.*

How are special effects accomplished? The best way is to hire professional special-effects people and stunt specialists who have experience in their fields. They are usually readily available, for a negotiated fee. Be sure to ask them for references and photos or movies of their work!

TWO DAYS IN THE LIFE OF YOUR PRODUCTION

Now for a couple of days in the life of your production. Let's say that your goal is to shoot about six to seven minutes of interior scenes for a ninety-minute film.

THE SCRIPT

Here is the situation we will be working with:

1. The seven minutes of eventual screentime that you will be filming deals with the eleventh through eighteenth minutes of your film.
2. In the first ten minutes of your movie, the following major characters have already been introduced:

April Springer:	16-year-old gymnast; America's hope to win the gold medal at the Olympics. She is sweet, naive, innocent. We are rooting for her all the way.
Jack Armstrong:	April's boyfriend, and schoolmate. A likeable, loyal, All-American kid.
Mrs. Springer:	April's mother. A "stage mother," always fussing over April and butting in on her work. She sees herself as a winner through April's talent.

Arnold Gary:	Coach of April's high school gymnastics team. A nice guy. He's got his hands full handling the pressures of being April's coach.
Mrs. Arnold Gary: (Zelda)	Very ambitious. Drives her husband to make the most of April's talent; she sees April's talent as a meal ticket to a bigger and better job for her husband. She wants success at any price.
Mr. Springer:	A middle-class business person who just wants the best for April. He leaves the business judgment about April's career to Mrs. Springer.
Dr. Arcane:	An egomaniacal doctor who performs experimental surgical transplants on people, using the tissues of monkeys. He'd sell anyone's soul including his own, to the devil, for glory. Once he gets his hands on you, you're sure to be a changed person.

Now, these are the seven minutes of script we will be filming:

INTERIOR   GYM   DAY

Sunlight streams through the gym windows, refracting bars of light and shadows on the equipment and polished amber floorboards. High school gymnasts and acrobats run, cartwheel, somersault and handspring through the several well-equipped areas containing bars, mats, horses, runways, beams and rings. Assistants and spotters hover over the kids, carefully coaching them. We hear various commands,

COMMANDS (o.s.)
    Wolf mount! Flank!
    Vault! Squat! Straddle!
as Jack Armstrong walks into the scene, with the loose gait and grace of an athlete. He has a pile of books and a lunch bag tucked under his arm.

INTERIOR   GYM   DAY   SAME TIME

Jack stops at the far end of the gym and, standing near the sidelines, surveys the scene. He is obviously blocking the view of a television technician who is wearing a headset, carrying a walkie-talkie and trying to operate some equipment on the floor, including a videotape recorder and television monitor on a dolly.

TECHNICIAN
    Hey kid, stand anywhere but there
JACK
    Oh, sorry...
Jack steps to his right, giving the Technician a clear view.
TECHNICIAN
    You on the team?
JACK
    Basketball team.
TECHNICIAN
    I mean this team, the gymnastic team...
    if you ain't, you gotta beat it.
    We start taping in a minute.

The Technician adjusts the TV monitor and we see a picture of the activity on the gym floor from the point of view of a camera on the other side of the gym.

JACK
    I'm waiting for my girl,
    April Springer.
TECHNICIAN
    April Springer? No kidding?....
    well, okay..., then you can stay here,
    but just stay out of the way.
Jack removes a chocolate bar from his lunch bag.
JACK
    You want some?
TECHNICIAN
    Don't mind if I do.

The Technician takes a piece of candy as a good-looking girl gymnast appears on his TV monitor and we hear over his walkie-talkie,

WALKIE-TALKIE
How's the signal over there?
The Technician stares at gymnast on the screen.
TECHNICIAN
Loud and clear

INTERIOR   GYM   SAME TIME

At the far side of the gym we see a full TV crew, with camera, lights and cables. The local TV personality, DAVID SHOESTRING, is sipping coffee and talking to ARNOLD GARY, Head Coach. They both walk toward the uneven parallel bars where the same attractive gymnast we saw on the monitor is doing floor exercises on a large mat.

INTERIOR   GYM   SAME TIME

As David and the Coach are walking, in the b.g. technicians are setting lights and dressing cable.

INTERIOR   GYM   SAME TIME

DAVID
Now then Coach, you do understand
how the sequence is to go?
COACH (adjusting walkie-talkie)
Oh sure, I've got it
DAVID
Well then, we're ready whenever
you and April are

INTERIOR   GYM'S LOCKER ROOM   SAME TIME

V.O. From walkie-talkie hooked on wall (Coach's voice)
Okay ladies, let's go

RUTH FLOWERS, April's Spotter and APRIL SPRINGER are together. April is on a dressing chair chalking her hands and Ruth is holding some chalk bags.
RUTH FLOWERS (into walkie-talkie)
We're on our way

Turns to April
      C'mon April, let's go
We hear a locker door closing o.s.

INTERIOR   GYM'S LOCKER ROOM   SAME TIME

MRS. SPRINGER enters the scene from behind a locker door,
laden with hairbrush, towel, lip-gloss and warm-up jacket.
      MRS. SPRINGER
      April...I don't want you to be nervous...
      just do a good job...everything will be fine
Mrs. Springer swarms over the quietly composed, docile April,
brushing her curly hair and forcing lip-gloss into her hands.
      MRS. SPRINGER
      Here...just a touch
      APRIL (flashing a smile)
      Okay, Mom.

INTERIOR   GYM'S LOCKER   SAME TIME

Obediently, April moves to a large mirror and applies the
lip-gloss. The mirror reflects a collection of newspaper and
magazine photo stories. Hand-lettered across the top of the
mirror we see, ON TO THE OLYMPICS! A prominent picture-
story about April is headlined: APRIL SPRINGER OUTSTANDING
GYMNAST—AMERICA'S #1 OLYMPIC HOPE.

INTERIOR   GYM'S LOCKER ROOM   SAME TIME

Mrs. Springer and Ruth Flowers wait for April as she gracefully
dips her slippered feet into the chalk box and rubs her hands.

INTERIOR   GYM'S LOCKER ROOM   SAME TIME

The trio stride toward the doorway exit. April is in the lead,
radiant and confident.

INTERIOR   GYM   SAME TIME

The Coach, David and some technicians are conferring as the
Coach spots the trio.

COACH
David, here they come
At the trio
C'mon Ruth! Let's move it!
The trio quickens their pace.

INTERIOR   GYM   SAME TIME

DAVID (his oily personality oozing)
Ah, April, delighted to meet you.
Your coach has been telling me
some fascinating things about you
April blushes.
What do you think about your
going to the Olympics?
APRIL
Oh, I think it's neat
DAVID
Are you excited?
Mrs. Springer walks into frame.
MRS. SPRINGER
Sure she is... but we've all
got our fingers crossed.
COACH
She's got to pass the trials first
DAVID
Well now, you and your coach have worked
out a dismount that's never been done
before... you *are* going to make it part of
the TV show for the folks here in your
hometown first, aren't you
APRIL
Sure, I mean, I don't know... I have to ask
(turning to Coach) Mr. Gary... Mr. Gary?
COACH
I don't know. I think we better...
no, we'd better wait on it...

David signals the technician to stop taping.

DAVID
Look Arnie, if she can do it, why not let
her do it? What'd we come out here for?
I mean, if you don't show the people
something newsworthy on the six o'clock news,
they'll fall asleep.

MRS. SPRINGER
He's right Arnie, and besides, it's
good public relations... good for you,
the town and April too

The Coach looks questioningly, first at Ruth, who shrugs, then at April.

APRIL
Please, Mr. Gary... it'll be alright

COACH
Okay

David quickly signals for the taping to begin as the mike is pinned to the Coach's collar.

INTERIOR   GYM   SAME TIME

April spots Jack Armstrong in the stands, waves merrily and he waves back. She then dashes to her starting position.

SAME TIME

April begins her routine. Everyone stops still. All eyes are on her.

SAME TIME

COACH (into mike) V.O. APRIL'S ACTION
April is tucking her legs in to gain momentum.
Now a stationary handstand... dropping onto two
giant swings, crossing her hands over and changing
direction... now she must speed up quickly...

CAMERA PERSON (whispers to David)
She's got a shadow on her

DAVID (whispers)
Turn the light in her direction

      LIGHTING TECHNICIAN
        Okay
Turns light

SAME TIME

The lighting pole is silently turned as the Coach, concentrating on April and, not noticing the lighting change, continues his running commentary.

      COACH
        ...she's gaining momentum
        for her dismount...

SAME TIME

April, about to dismount, is blinded by the bright beam of the powerful lights. She hesitates, releases too soon, falls out of control, missing the mats, crashing to the floor, her right shoulder hitting hard.

SAME TIME

Dead silence. Everyone is stunned. A scream pierces the air. It is Mrs. Springer. The Coach is the first to move as feet and faces flash by. April is crying.

      RUTH FLOWERS
        Get an ambulance!
She runs to April, followed by the Coach

      COACH
        Get a doctor, quick!
      RUTH
        I'll get a stretcher
She dashes off

      DAVID (unctuously, to Mrs. Springer)
        There's a specialist at our studio today...
        I'll have a technician call and
        get him here...his name's Dr. Arcane...

CUT

SCRIPT BREAKDOWN

Break the following script down into its component parts. The first task is what is commonly called the assistant director's script breakdown.

The terms used in the script breakdown are defined as follows:

Production title: *The April Springer Story* is the working title of the movie.

Location: The physical address of the location at which you'll be filming.

Set: The setting in which the scene will be filmed.

Sequence: A short title for a sequence; a single unit of related scenes.

Period: The time frame in which the action takes place.

Season: The time of the year in which the action takes place.

Day or night: The time of the day in which the action takes place.

Total script pages: The number of pages in your script that cover the scenes for this set and sequence.

Cast: A list of lead and supporting cast in the scenes.

Bits: A list of distinguishable minor characters.

Extras: Nonspeaking, background actors.

Process-effects, construction: A listing of special requirements for the scenes to be filmed.

Music-misc.:   Music, background and other audio effects that occur in the scenes.

Props-action props, animals: A list of essential props for the action occurring in the scenes.

Scene numbers & synopsis: Scene numbers as they appear in the script and sufficient detail for those working in the scenes to understand them; usually the salient point of each scene.

SCRIPT BREAKDOWN

PRODUCTION TITLE		LOCATION
THE APRIL SPRINGER STORY		(Address of Gymnasium)

SET	SEQUENCE	April prepares for Olympic
Locker Room		routine; part of accident sequence

PERIOD	SEASON	DAY	NIGHT	TOTAL SCRIPT PAGES
Contemporary	Spring	X		1½

CAST	BITS	SCENE NUMBERS & SYNOPSIS
April Springer Mrs. Springer Ruth Flowers	None	4) Ruth Flowers responds to walkie-talkie. 5) Mrs. Springer & Ruth Flowers attend to April in locker room. 6) Mirror reveals press notices for April. 7) April chalks up and the three of them exit the locker room.
	EXTRAS None	

PROCESS–EFFECTS–CONSTRUCTION
None

MUSIC–MISCELLANEOUS

PROPS–ACTION PROPS–ANIMALS
Chalk and chalk bags.
Small hand-lettered banner:
On to The Olympics.

Newspaper and Magazine
photo-stories about April.

Walkie-talkie, table,
mirror, chair.

SCRIPT BREAKDOWN

PRODUCTION TITLE		LOCATION
THE APRIL SPRINGER STORY		(Address of Gymnasium)

SET	SEQUENCE	
Gymnasium	April's Accident	

PERIOD	SEASON	DAY	NIGHT	TOTAL SCRIPT PAGES
Contemporary	Spring	X		6

CAST	BITS	SCENE NUMBERS & SYNOPSIS
April Springer Jack Armstrong Mrs. Springer Coach Arnold Gary Ruth Flowers David Shoe- string	TV Monitor Technician Lighting Technician Camera Operator	1) Gymnasts practicing in gym. 2) Jack Armstrong enters gym, talks with TV Technician.

BITS

TV Monitor Technician

Lighting Technician

Camera Operator

EXTRAS

3 TV Technicians

2 Assistant Coaches

2 Spotters

10 Gymnasts

SCENE NUMBERS & SYNOPSIS

1) Gymnasts practicing in gym.

2) Jack Armstrong enters gym, talks with TV Technician.

3) TV Technicians set up equipment, and David and the Coach talk.

8) April, Mrs. Springer and Ruth enter gym.

9) David interviews April, who agrees to perform her Olympic routine.

10) April spots Jack Armstrong.

11) April performs her routine and has accident.

12) The call for medical help.

PROCESS–EFFECTS–CONSTRUCTION

Special Effects: Rigging, so that April can perform her own stunt.

Construction: Staging around the uneven parallel bars, for camera; scaffolding.

MUSIC–MISCELLANEOUS

Record sound effects, walkie-talkie effects, voice-overs, ambient sounds of gymnasts.

Music: Background music for floor routines.

PROPS–ACTION PROPS–ANIMALS

Gym equipment including mats for tumbling, ropes, bars, vaulting horses, balance beam.

TV equipment, including camera, monitor, VTR, lights, cables, headsets; detail with prop person.

FLOOR PLANS

To film the script, we must convert it into a kind of architectural rendering or road map, so to speak. We must therefore draw up the following floor plan for the action in the gym. Using this plan as a model, you might try drawing up the one for the locker room, as an exercise. Not only is it necessary but, you'll get involved and have fun doing it too!

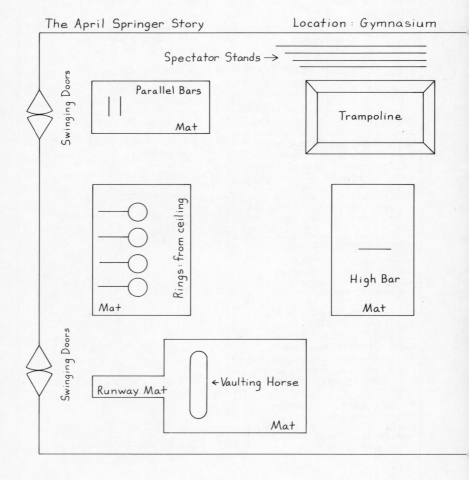

Door

← Spectator Stands

Uneven parallel bars

Runway Mat

Mat

Balance Beams

Tumbling Mat

Mat

Vaulting Horse→

Runway Mat

Mat

SHOT LIST

A shot list is a listing of every shot to be filmed in every scene to be filmed. Here is a suggested shot list for the shooting of April's Accident and the Locker Room. Please refer to the Scene Numbers.

APRIL'S ACCIDENT

Scene Number	Shot List
1 ---------1	Wide shot of gymnasts in gym
1 ---------2	Shot of girls on balance beam
1 ---------3	Pan shot of girls on vaulting horse
1 ---------4	Shot of boys and girls on trampoline
1 ---------5	Shot of boys on vaulting horse
2 ---------1	Dolly shot of Jack's entrance
2 ---------2	Shot of Jack and Technician One
2 ---------3	Shot of TV monitor from Technician One's POV
2 ---------4	Shot of Jack, Technician One & TV monitor
3 ---------1	Shot of David Shoestring and Coach Gary, attractive gymnast in foreground and technicians in background
3 ---------2	Attractive gymnast on TV monitor
8 ---------1	Shot of April, Mrs. Springer and Ruth Flowers entering gym
8 ---------2	Shot of April, Mrs. Springer, Ruth Flowers, David and Coach at uneven parallel bars
9 ---------1	Shot of David
9 ---------2	Shot of April
9 ---------3	Shot of Mrs. Springer into frame with April
9 ---------4	Group shot of April, Mrs. Springer, Coach and David
9 ---------5	Shot of David, then Mrs. Springer into frame
9 ---------6	Group shot of April, Coach, Mrs. Springer and David favoring April and Coach
9 ---------7	Group shot of April, Mrs. Springer, Coach and David favoring April and Mrs. Springer
9 ---------8	Group shot of April, Mrs. Springer, Coach and David, favoring April

9 ---------9   Dolly shot of April leaving group
9 --------10   Shot of April, then pull back to reveal all eyes on April
10 --------1   Insert shot of Jack in gym from April's POV
11 --1 to 15   Fifteen shots of April's routine and reaction shots to it, including some subjective shots from April's POV (for example, her hands firmly gripping the bars, outstretched arms, her crash and fall)
12 --------1   Group shot of Coach, Mrs. Springer & David as Coach runs to April
12 --------2   April on ground with Ruth Flowers
12 --------3   Coach and April; Ruth exits
12 --------4   David and Mrs. Springer; TV camera operator in b.g.

LOCKER ROOM

Scene Number	Shot List
4 ---------1	Ruth Flowers and April Springer
5 ---------1	Mrs. Springer, then pan as she joins April and Ruth
5 ---------2	April
6 ---------1	April to mirror
6 ---------2	Articles taped to mirror
6 ---------3	April at mirror with Mrs. Springer
7 ---------1	April chalks up as Mrs. Springer and Ruth Flowers stand by, then all three walk out the door

You are faced with completing fifty shots in two days of work. In addition, remember that you're unlikely to get what you want on the first take of each shot. Budget your time for the two sequences so that you figure on between four and ten takes for each shot. Just how many hours will all these shots take?

Let's break them down further into a shooting schedule so that we can check how reasonable an estimate of work time you have made.

For efficiency, you should consolidate your action by shooting area by area by area on your two sets—the Gym and the Locker Room:

I. Overall Action in Gym

Scene	Shot
1	1
1	2
1	3
1	4
1	5
2	1
8	1

II. Jack & Technician One by the Spectator Stands - Gym

2	2
2	3
2	4
10	1

III. Area of Uneven Parallel Bars - Gym

3	1
3	2
8	2
9	1 to 10
11	1 to 15
12	1 to 4

IV. Locker Room
All shots in one group

A consideration for Area I: Under this group you have five shots for Scene One. You'll need to light a large area—the entire gym. It will take lots of personnel and lights. Remember, this scene could possibly take five hours to work through. (The only way to accurately judge how long it will take is to test your crew out prior to production. Have them simulate set-ups, like the war maneuvers of naval personnel on a ship of the fleet.) Such a long shooting period means that, if you start shooting at 7 a.m. and finish at noon, it will have to look like 7 a.m. for five hours.

Therefore, if you cannot shoot this scene with available light and *push* the film in this kind of low-light situation, you should probably omit this scene, which is not necessary to the plot in any case. The film you're using has an ASA rating of 100; you can push it to 200, perhaps 400. Of course, pushing the film almost always means less image quality. So, unless it's economically sound both money- and time-wise, definitely think about scratching Scene One and all its five shots.

Here's a possible schedule for both days requiring twelve or thirteen hours work on the first day, and seventeen to nineteen hours on the second day.

First Day

Scene	Shot
1	1
1	2
1	3
1	4
1	5

Then set up for shots involving Jack Armstrong,

2	1	Long dolly shot

Then, break for lunch; then,

1	2	these two shots
[8	1]	are tied together

Then, all Locker Room shots—
that is, all shots in scenes 4, 5, 6, and 7

Then, before calling it a day, pre-light the area around the uneven parallel bars for the next day's work.

Second Day

Scene	Shot
2	2
2	3
2	4

Scene	Shot
3	1
3	2
8	2
9	all
10	1
11	all
12	all

A major company would take three days to film what you must in two days. The major company roughly figures on getting two minutes of screen time each day of production. An independent, however, should figure on at least three minutes of screen time per day.

STORY BOARD

Now you return to the floor plan for the Gymnasium (page 150) and if you've drawn it, the one of the Locker Room as well. Using these floor plans you diagram the action and camera placement to get the right shots for your scenes. After you've decided on placement, according to the way you want to see the movie directed, you'll probably review and revise your shot list and floor plans for directional continuity. After this has been fully discussed and decided upon, the next step is to draw a story board for each and every scene and each and every shot in every scene. At right is an example for Scene 2, Shot 1.

MAKING IT

Once you have done the story board, think about how to minimize set-ups for your camera positions so you will know exactly the positioning of the camera to get your shots down pat, in shooting order. You will probably try to film all group shots as one master shot and intercut your close-ups in the editing. That means that when you shoot your close-ups, you will have to make sure that people are saying the same thing they said in the master group shots, and that the lighting and sounds match exactly, as well. For example, if swinging gymnasts are swinging

SCENE NUMBER: 2	SCRIPT PAGES: 14
SHOT NUMBER: 1	

DIRECTION (ACTION): Medium wide shot of Jack Armstrong entering gymnasium. Camera dollies with him as he crosses the gym, then stops and stands in front of Technician One near the spectator stands.

DIALOGUE: Voice-over by Technician One at end of shot.

BLOCKING (SCREEN DIRECTION): Jack enters facing camera, turns to walk screen left to right, crosses in front of Technician One and stops Screen Right.

CAMERA ACTION:

Medium Wide Shot

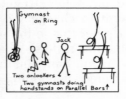

Medium Wide Shot

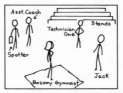

Medium Wide Shot

LIGHTING:	EFFECTS:	SOUND:
Natural Lighting, if possible. (See later discussion.)	None	Ambient sounds in gym and low-key coaching commands.

on the ropes in the background of your master shot, then they will have to swing exactly the same way if they are in a cutaway close-up or medium shot. You'll also want to have several books on gymnastics so that the scenes involving gymnastics play as realistically as possible.

You will be getting ideas about your script and the way you want to film it as you work. You may need a professional choreographer to help frame the action in the gym. Sketch every shot, probably on 5″ x 8″ cards, and pin them up on a wall to get a "picture" of how things will look on-screen when you finally shoot your scene. They are like frames from your planned movie. These cards also help you to "hook" or "tag" one shot to another. For example, the attractive gymnast first appears on Technician One's TV monitor. Then you cut to the area around the uneven parallel bars where the same gymnast is tumbling on the mat. Look for gaps and holes in the visual, and make adjustments along the way—planned adjustments!

You may, as we discussed earlier, drop the entire Scene One because it may be impractical to film. As a working substitute, you can establish the gym as Jack walks into it. The point is constantly to ask yourself just what is essential for you to film? It will almost always come down to, "What is essential to the story?" If you don't have the time to get a shot you want, but it isn't essential to the story, you may have to drop it in the interest of time and budget requirements. To get at what is essential to the story you may want to change the scene with Jack and Technician One. Remember that in the script Jack doesn't run over to April when she suffers what appears to be a career-ending injury. Do you want him to run to her? You'll be deciding on all these things, depending on your vision of the movie you are filming.

In striving for essential action, you will want to accentuate the strong action scenes to give them a feeling of urgency with which the audience can empathize when the film is completed. April's fall, for example, is a stunt that needs careful planning. You should think about putting a belt around her waist and stringing her up with invisible wires to a pulley on the ceiling of the gym. You may want to shoot this scene with three cameras. One at normal speed, twenty-four frames a second; the second camera at eighteen frames a second, to speed up the action; the third camera at eighty frames a second, to give you slow-motion shots. Later, you and the editor can decide on just what works for you in the editing room where you are likely to be for several months. Scenes 9, 11 and 12, also require very careful planning and many rehearsals.

To create suspense you may write in some foreboding of things to come in your early scenes in the gym. For example, in the background, a gymnast could fall and hurt herself or almost hurt herself. Or someone could be talking about how dangerous April's upcoming stunt really is. How effective is such tele-graphing of the point of the scene? Only you can decide.

It is essential that the director should be thinking through all the possibilities *prior* to the actual shoot. He or she must have in mind not only an exact picture of what is desired on the screen but also an inner-ear and inner-eye 'feeling' for the real pace and rhythm to his or her work, as we discussed in Chapter One.

The results of your work will, of course, be reflected in the dailies (rushes) you get back from the lab. But even then you cannot and should not judge your potential movie fully from the dailies. You can always use opticals, for stop action and freezes or for speed up of the action during the editing and at the optical house later on. So the director should stage all the action in the gym and make sure that it is all relevant to what he or she wants, knowing that changes will be made later.

After the day's shooting is over, you make up your camera and sound reports and send them to the labs together with the negative you shot that day. That night you will spend several hours filling out your production reports. Remember, we warned you that most movies made by independents are never finished. You should be in great physical shape to endure on location about four to five weeks, six days a week because you might only expect to sleep four or five hours a day, day after day. You will be burning lots of energy between the emotional and physical pressures of the work but you always have the dailies to look forward to. They'll be back from the lab in the next day or two and you'll be seeing the gym scene and the locker room scene. Do they look the way you wanted them to? When you screen your *dailies*, you don't invite anyone but your immediate production team to the screening. Dailies, or "rushes," the film you shot yesterday and sent to the lab for processing, are for you and the producer, the director, and the camera and lighting departments to study. Dailies are not color corrected, and they're one-light prints. They're boring. They are repetitious. They are learning documents. Maybe your good screenplay just isn't translating into a movie. You may want to scrap the whole production effort right then and there. Or you might want to make some changes. Or you might want to see if your cameras are in focus, that your lighting is working, that you're getting the action angles and visuals that you intended to get and thought you were getting. So, dailies are like spot exams. They're working proofs of your film, and you should use them to seek answers.

Don't allow actors to see the dailies, if at all possible. They are likely to be highly emotional about it. They may even start acting a different way as a result of being personally dissatisfied with their performances in the dailies. You don't want them to unilaterally alter their acting styles! That should come from their director.

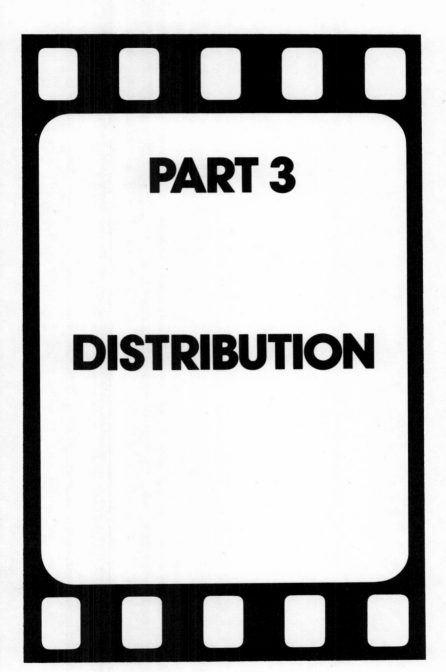

PART 3

DISTRIBUTION

CHAPTER 9

DISTRIBUTION: THE MIDDLEMAN

Distribution is the key pillar of the Production-Distribution-Exhibition troika. Distributors deal with both producers and exhibitors. Once your movie is completed, you will offer it to a distributor.

Why? What do distribution companies do? They acquire movies from producers. They lease these movies to exhibitors.

Distributors:

- create and control the leasing of movies to theaters

- create and control advertising campaigns

- create and control publicity, exploitation and promotional devices to push their product

- are the marketing branch of the industry. They merchandise the movies. They make them merchandisable for the public. Their campaigns may not have anything to do with the story or theme of your movie. These campaigns are based on their perceptions of what must be done to sell the exhibitors, the critics, the opinion-makers, and the public on your movie.

- are businesspeople, vendors, salespeople, spielers, negotiators, dealers, traders, amateur psychologists, merchants, higglers, hucksters, fakers, agents, sales engineers, tradespeople, manipulators, hawkers, auctioneers, high-pressure power-brokers—in short, the rascally knaves to whom everyone in the motion picture industry entrusts his or her future.

- are single-minded in purpose. Their point of view is that they have *products* to sell. These products are movies, supposedly works of art but distributors take these products, and through a series of commercial actions, try to convert them into money. Real money. A distributor's fealty is to profits alone. Nothing else matters. Just mazuma, simoleons, shekels, gold and silver, wampum, bucks and bullion.

- are pragmatists. The first question they ask of themselves when they see your movie is: "Will it make money or, won't it?" NOT "Is it a good movie or, isn't it?"

ORGANIZING THE MARKETPLACE

Distributors have their home offices in New York or Los Angeles and branch offices in various major cities in the United States and Canada. They call these cities "exchange cities." In the early days of the business, exhibitors would exchange money for a print of a movie. Offices were usually near bus depots or train stations to facilitate travel and shipments. Today, they're usually located in modern office buildings, and each office generally has from three to twenty employees, depending upon how much business it does. Each exchange city has one or more key cities, including the exchange city. Sometimes key cities are referred to as chart towns. They are the cities that render the most film rentals, in aggregate.

The table below shows the way distributors divide the United States and Canada. Note that in several cities, for example, Buffalo, most distributors have a branch there to cover both the Buffalo and Albany exchanges, but a few may have an office in both cities. In addition, I have listed the approximate percentage of annual U.S. and Canadian film rentals that each exchange city usually accounts for in a given year. Of course, these percentages may vary from company to company and from movie to movie. Some movies may do better in a certain exchange territory or region of the country. For example, a Woody Allen movie will do better in New York than Oklahoma City. An automobile racing movie is likely to do better in Charlotte than Boston. So please use the percentages only as a working guideline, a composite picture of the sort of return you might be looking for if you had ten to twenty movies a year to distribute, all of them with different themes, budgets, stars, directors, writers, producers, and stories.

KEY CITIES

Exchange City (and geographic area)	Key Cities	Approximate aggregate percentage of total U.S. and Canadian movie rentals
ATLANTA ...Alabama, Georgia, Tennessee east of the Tennessee River	Atlanta, Athens, Augusta, Birmingham, Chattanooga, Columbus, Knoxville, Macon, Montgomery, Nashville, Savannah	3.57
BOSTON (NEW HAVEN) ...Maine, eastern Massachusetts New Hampshire, Rhode Island, Eastern Vermont; Connecticut	Boston, Brockton, Lawrence, Portland, Providence, Worcester New Haven, Bridgeport Hartford, Stamford	5.77
BUFFALO (ALBANY) ...Upper New York State, western Vermont, western Massachusetts; western New York State	Buffalo, Albany, Binghampton, Rochester, Syracuse, Utica	2.0

CHARLOTTE
...North Carolina and   Charlotte, Charleston,   2.8
South Carolina   Columbia, Durham,
                            Fayetteville, Greensboro,
                            Raleigh, Winston-Salem

CHICAGO
...Northern Illinois,   Chicago, Champaign,   3.32
part of Indiana and   Joliet, Peoria,
Upper Michigan   Rockford, South Bend,
                            Waukegan

CINCINNATI
...Southern Ohio, parts   Cincinnati, Columbus,   2.5
of Kentucky, West Virginia Dayton, Lexington
and Indiana

CLEVELAND
...Northern half of Ohio   Cleveland, Akron,   1.75
                            Canton, Toledo,
                            Youngstown

DALLAS
...Texas and parts of   Dallas, Albuquerque,   6.5
Oklahoma, New Mexico,   Austin, Corpus Christi,
Louisiana, Arkansas and   El Paso, Fort Worth,
Arizona   Houston, San Antonio

DENVER
...Colorado, western Nebraska, Denver, Boulder,   2.3
part of New Mexico and   Colorado Springs, Pueblo
Wyoming, and Black Hills
of South Dakota

DES MOINES (OMAHA)
...Parts of Iowa, Missouri,   Des Moines,
Minnesota and Illinois;   Cedar Rapids,   1.57
western Iowa, most of Nebraska, Davenport, Iowa City,
part of Minnesota   Lincoln, Omaha,
                            Sioux City

DETROIT
...Lower peninsula of   Detroit, Ann Arbor,   4.25
Michigan and parts of   Flint, Grand Rapids,
Indiana   Lansing, Pontiac

INDIANAPOLIS

...Most of Indiana and
western half of Kentucky

Indianapolis, Bloomington, Evansville, Fort Wayne, Kokomo, Lafayette, Louisville, Terre Haute	1.73

JACKSONVILLE

...Florida

Jacksonville, Daytona Beach, Fort Lauderdale, Hollywood, Miami, Miami Beach, Coral Gables, Orlando, Sarasota, St. Petersburg, Tampa	4.0

KANSAS CITY

...Kansas, western Missouri,
parts of Nebraska, Oklahoma,
Arkansas and Ouisiana

Kansas City, Topeka, Wichita	1.93

LOS ANGELES

...Southern California, parts
of Arizona, New Mexico and
Nevada

Los Angeles, Las Vegas, Phoenix, San Diego, Tucson	10.00

MILWAUKEE

...Upper peninsula of
Michigan and most of
Wisconsin

Milwaukee, Appleton, Green Bay, Madison	1.20

MINNEAPOLIS

...Parts of Iowa, Minnesota,
Montana, North Dakota,
Wisconsin and South Dakota
except Black Hills section

Minneapolis, Fargo, Rochester, St. Paul	2.0

NEW ORLEANS (MEMPHIS)

...Louisiana, parts of Mississippi,
Alabama, Arkansas, Florida;
northern Mississippi, western
Tennessee, part of Kentucky
and Missouri

New Orleans, Baton Rouge, Ft. Smith, Jackson, Miss., Lake Charles, Little Rock, Memphis, Mobile, Pensacola, Shreveport	3.59

NEW YORK
...Long Island, Greater New
York City, New York State
as far as Poughkeepsie
and northern New Jersey

New York, Asbury Park,   8.0
Bayonne, Brooklyn,
Elizabeth, Englewood,
Jersey City, Kingston,
Middletown, Newark,
New Brunswick,
Newburgh, Passaic,
Paterson, Perth Amoby,
Plainfield, Poughkeepsie

OKLAHOMA CITY
...Oklahoma, parts of
Arkansas and Texas

Oklahoma City,   1.67
Lubbock, Tulsa

PHILADELPHIA
...Most of Delaware, southern
New Jersey and eastern
Pennsylvania

Philadelphia, Camden,   3.58
Harrisburg, Norristown,
Princeton, Trenton,
Wilmington

PITTSBURGH
...Western Pennyvania
and part of West Virginia

Pittsburgh, Erie,   1.33
Morgantown, Sharon,
State College, Wheeling

ST. LOUIS
...Northern Arkansas, small
part of Kentucky, southern
Illinois and eastern Missouri

St. Louis, Cape Girard,   1.70
Quincy, Springfield, Ill.

SALT LAKE CITY
...Parts of Arizona, Idaho,
Nevada, Wyoming, Oregon,
Montana and Utah

Salt Lake City, Boise,   1.88
Ogden, Provo

SAN FRANCISCO
...Northern California,
Nevada, southern Oregon
and Hawaii

San Francisco, Fresno,   5.0
Honolulu, Oakland,
Sacramento, San Jose

SEATTLE (PORTLAND)
...Washington, Alaska and part
of Idaho, parts of Idaho
California and Washington

Seattle, Anchorage,   3.2
Eugene, Portland,
Spokane

WASHINGTON, D.C.		
...District of Columbia, small section of Delaware, Maryland, Virginia and part of West Virginia	Washington, D.C., Baltimore, Newport News, Norfolk, Richmond	3.6
	TOTAL U.S.A.	91.74%
CANADA		
Calgary	Calgary, Edmonton	1.05
Montreal	Montreal, Quebec City	1.35
St. John	St. John, Halifax	.50
Toronto	Toronto	3.4
Vancouver	Vancouver	1.1
Winnepeg	Winnepeg	.86
	TOTAL CANADA	8.26%
COMBINED U.S.A. and CANADA		**100.00%**

THE MAJORS

A major motion picture production-distribution company is usually defined as a member of the Motion Picture Association of America (MPAA). These members include:

Allied Artists   Paramount
Avco-Embassy   Twentieth Century Fox
Buena Vista   United Artists
(The distribution arm of Disney) Universal
Columbia   Warner Bros.

MGM, also an MPAA member, currently distributes its productions through United Artists, and the recent major entry into production, Orion Pictures, has stated it intends to distributed its product, at least for a while, through Warner Bros. In addition, the above nine producing-distributing companies do serve as acquiring-distributing companies. On occasion, they do acquire movies made by independents for distribution.

However, for the most part, they distribute movies that are financed in-house. Sometimes they band together and finance bits and pieces of one another's movies. Perhaps one company will distribute a given movie in the United States and Canada and another will distribute that same movie overseas ("offshore)." As a guess, I'd say that the above companies do 85 percent of the world's movie business, even though they distribute only seventy-five to 100 new films a year, more or less. All of them have branch offices with salaried employees.

THE MINOR MAJORS, MAJOR MINORS, AND OTHER "INDIES"

Independent distributors are sometimes called "states-righters", because they contract for franchises to distribute movies outside the major company structure on a state-by-state or territory-by-territory basis. The parent organization usually has a home office in New York or Los Angeles.

The individual franchise holders have offices in the same branch cities as the majors, except that these franchise holders receive commissions for distributing movies, not a salary and bonus. Their commission usually ranges from 10 to 50 percent of the film rental collected from each playdate. The percentage is 25 percent. These local franchise holders, in effect, run their own business; they are independent business people, usually representing one to a dozen or more independent producing-acquiring-distributing companies. An example of some of the more active independents who supply product to states-righters are:

American International (the only distributor in this group to have salaried exchange personnel rather than commission franchise holders)	Compass International
	Crown International
	Dimension Pictures
	Film Ventures
	Group One
	Key International
Atlantic Releasing	International Picture Show
Joseph Brenner	New Line
Brut	New World
Cinema Shares	World Northal

If you arrange for any of these companies to handle your movie in the U.S. and Canada, you'll probably have to make separate deals for all offshore distribution, since most independent distributors have no direct overseas involvements. A few have, from time to time, of course. It's also possible that you might make a deal with a major company to handle your film overseas and an independent one to distribute it domestically. Perhaps the major might think your movie is an exploitation, low-budgeter that an independent could do better with domestically; however, the major might see it as having broad appeal as an export item.

Obviously, there are many more independents than majors that come and go at any one time. Success for many "indies" can be just one film that does a lot of business. Yet there are another hundred or so indies with products to sell. As you can see, life for the indies is full of uncertainties and gambles.

THE HIGH COSTS OF ADVERTISING

If a distributor decides to take on your film, then it is prepared to take some risks and to do its best to make money in the market.

There are many expenses involved in promoting your film. The distributor may decide that the way to distribute your movie is to order 200 release prints. At current prices, that's a cost of about $150,000. The distributor will conceptualize advertising campaigns, design press material and produce trailers. Those items cost another $75,000. Shipping of items is an additional expense. There may also be special give-away and merchandizing campaigns, trade ads and exhibitor screenings. That could add another $25,000. Then, the distributor could round up 200 theaters across the country, or in one region of the nation, to premiere your film. TV advertising is especially expensive, ranging from $20,000 to $150,000 for each TV spot. Many popular shows cost about $75,000 for each spot commercial. Just ten of these commercials can equal the cost of your movie.

Remember, your film, which cost a hypothetical $750,000, is your business. The distributor will have to take into consideration all the above costs as necessary to maximize every potential seen in your movie.

TURN IT OVER

Here's what you must have ready to present to the distributor, if you want to make a deal:

1. One fully timed color-corrected 35mm answer print with synchronous optical sound track.
2. Internegative of textless main and end title background.
3. Main and end titles.
4. One 35mm reversal internegative of the TV version of the picture that meets U.S. television network continuity acceptance standards, fully cut, edited and assembled with sound track in synchronization therewith. (Ideally your movie will be sold to a TV network after its theatrical runs.)
5. One 35 mm magnetic sound track containing separate magnetic striping of the music only, separate striping containing each and every sound effect contained in the sound track, separate striping of the dialogue, and in the event of any musical vocal renditions, a separate striping of them.
6. Dialogue continuity.
7. Music cue sheets; lead sheets, 7½-speed and ¼-inch tapes.
8. Original negatives and six positive prints of not less than one hundred still photographs, 8″ x 10″ each (for pressbooks and newspaper publicity).
9. A statement of credits to be accorded all persons related to the film.
10. Biographical information on the leading members of the cast and crew.
11. Notes and stories about the production; intended as publicity.
12. All outtakes of the movie.

THREE TYPES OF DISTRIBUTION DEALS

Arranging for distribution can be a Brave New World for any filmmaker. You are already exhausted from your production efforts, and now you're under the gun to get the movie distributed. It's a time to call up your emotional and intellectual reserves, and possibly, a business advisor and/or attorney. It's rare indeed for creative people to negotiate business dealings concerning their own output in an effective manner. I suggest a stand-in, experienced in negotiating, who knows exactly what you want for your movie. If the person in charge of distribution is interested in your film, a company attorney will join in drawing up an agreement. Words have legal definitions that are often quite different from their everyday usage and definitions. None of this relieves you of your obligation to make all business decisions in a clear-headed, mature fashion. Those who shirk this responsibility may get their movie distributed, but get little or no reasonable opportunity of earning monies from percentages.

There are hundreds of types of distribution deals. Here are three typical ones:

A. Distributor gives you an advance of $375,000 for the movie, against percentages of the profits.
B. Distributor offers to buy your film for $1 million outright.
C. Distributor gives you no money in advance but offers a deal whereby you have a chance to earn money based on percentages of the net profit.

Here are some terms you will be dealing with in negotiating your agreement:

Gross film rentals: The amount paid to the distributor by the exhibitor for exhibition of a movie. For example, if the distributor charges a film 50% and the theater grosses $10,000 at the box office, then the box-office gross is $10,000 and the gross film rental is $5,000.

Distribution fees: The amount of money, based on percentages, that the distributor is allowed to retain from the gross film rentals—usually 30 percent. For example, 30 percent of the $5,000 or, $1,500.

So far your accounting would look like this:

Box-office gross	$10,000
Gross film rental (50 %)	5,000
Less distribution fee (30%)	1,500
Amount remaining	$3,500

There are further costs to be charged against this amount for direct distribution expenses, ususally including the following items: recoupment of print costs; recoupment of shipping costs; recoupment of all advertising costs of any kind. You should also include here *any* expense incurred in distributing the movie, unless you expressly define precise items as nondeductible. Then, after all the deductions, you get 50 percent and the distribution company gets 50 percent.

Let's see how this works in Deal A. Suppose you invested $750,000 in making a movie and got a $375,000 advance against percentages.

HYPOTHETICAL NATIONAL DISTRIBUTION

U.S box-office gross	$5,000,000
Gross film rental (50%)	2,500,000
Less distribution fee (30 %)	750,000
Less hypothetical direct distribution costs	625,000
Less recoupment of advance	375,000
Amount remaining	750,000
You get 50%	$ 375,000
Distributor gets	$ 375,000

Add the $375,000 recoupment of advance and your $375,000 share of the amount remaining. This totals $750,000. You are now even on your original investment. That's an accomplishment!

To do that, your movie had to gross five million dollars at the theater box offices. With ticket prices at about $2.50 per capita, two million people had to see the movie. You can see that making a movie that's a personal statement for friends and family and one's own ego just doesn't work in this real world.

But, cheer up. The distributor may make a TV network deal. That can be anywhere from about $500,000 on up. Half of that should be yours, in this "guesstimate" example distribution agreement.

You can also make money on your movie without a TV network deal. Using the same example above, suppose your movie grosses $6 million instead of $5 million. In that case, the figures would look like this:

U.S. box-office gross	$6,000,000
Gross film rental (50%)	3,000,000
Less distribution fee (30%)	900,000
Less hypothetical direct distribution costs	625,000
Less recoupment of advance	375,000
Amount remaining	$1,100,000
You get 50%	$550,000
Distributor gets	$550,000

In this example, you are now in a profit position to the tune of $175,000.

If for example, you sold the movie outright to the distributor, as in Deal B, for whatever the figure, the distributor would keep all revenue. Of course, it's a gamble both ways, since the movie may flop and you'd end up with your money and the distributor would have to absorb all losses.

In a variation on Deal A, you might suggest to the distribution company the following:

1. You get $250,000 cash advance
2. The distributor retains 70 percent of the gross film rental and pays all costs
3. You receive 30 percent of all gross film rentals without any deductions

Suppose in this example your movie grossed $5 million in theaters. Here's how the figures would look:

U.S. box-office gross	$5,000,000
Gross film rental (50%)	$2,500,000
You get 30% of $2,500,000	$ 750,000

Subtract $250,000 advance you've already received, so you end up with $500,000.

You're even on your investment!

In this case, you probably won't get an accounting, unless your contract specifies that the distributor spend certain minimums on prints and advertising, out of the direct distribution costs. The disadvantage of this arrangement is that you will never know how hard the distributor tried to get playdates and good terms from theaters, unless this is specifically detailed in your contract. In any event, it's an old formula that works for some producers.

Of course, if the movie grosses $100,000,000 it is likely to command higher film rentals. The way film rentals work out nowadays, the more the movie grosses at the box office, the greater the percentage of every dollar taken in at the theater goes to the distributor. That 50 percent rental, whereby the distributor gets half of every buck that comes into the theater box office, could rise to 55 to 70 percent, or more. Therefore, you set the stage for windfall profits to distributor and moviemaker, as well. We will discuss this situation in greater detail in Part Four: Exhibition.

You might ask why the distributor gets 30 percent right off the top of every dollar in film rental. After all, literary agents only get 10 percent. But distribution just isn't that rational a game. The distributor solicits playdates from exhibitors, books and ships movies, and secures box-office statements. Most important, the distributor *collects film rentals* from exhibitors. If you went about distributing your own movie, armed with all the knowledge about the exchange cities and key cities, everything might go well until it came time for you to collect film rentals due you. Without another movie or a continued flow of movies, you would have a very difficult time collecting film rentals from exhibitors in faraway places. You would probably end up paying a collection agency 50 percent to enforce collection. The distributor plays a valuable role in enforcing film rental collection. In Deal C, the producer earns money solely from percentage of the net profit.

Here are three examples of the way these big-budget deals look. Suppose that the budget for your movie is $7 million, that the production-distribution company puts up all the money, and you put together all the talent. But, this time you've got high-priced talent. Suppose your number one star gets 15 percent of the producer's net receipts; star number two gets 10 percent of the producer's net receipts; the director get 5 percent of the producer's net receipts. Then, the screenwriter gets 10 percent of whatever the amount is after all of the above people; in other words, the screenwriter gets 10 percent of the net. You, the producer, also get 10 percent of the net.

HYPOTHETICAL EXAMPLE ONE

U.S. box-office receipts (amount paid by patrons at theaters)	$25,000,000
Less gross film rental (60%)	15,000,000
Less distribution fee (30% of Gross Film Rental)	4,500,000
Less direct distribution costs (mostly prints, shipping & advertising)	2,350,000

So far we have to deduct $6,850,000 from $15,000,000. This leaves a balance of $8,150,000. Let's call this figure the net gross.

Now, from the net gross of $8,150,000 we deduct the cost of the investment in the production, which the production-distribution company is entitled to recoup because that's what it cost to make the movie. If this cost is $7 million, we have a balance, or profit, of $1,150,000. This figure is also called the producer's a net receipts.

Star number one receives 15% of $1,150,000	$172,500
Star number two receives 10%	115,000
Director receives 5%	57,500
Total third-party shares (30%)	345,000
Net profit after third-party deductions	805,000
Writer receives 10% of the net profit	80,500
Producer receives 10% of the net profit	80,500

This leaves an amount of $634,000 called the net net. It is disbursed to any and all who had "pieces" of the film's net net profits.

The people who might have these "pieces" are the executive producer that the production company assigned to the movie to watch over the production; the assistant producer; lesser stars and feature players; the assistant director, camera operator; director of photography; and perhaps the banks who supplied the money to produce the movie.

HYPOTHETICAL EXAMPLE TWO

Suppose you have managed to secure the services of a really big name star. This star wants and get 10 percent of the amount of money remaining after the distributor's fee has been deducted from the gross film rental. Everything else is the same as in Example One.

U.S. Box-office receipts	$25,000,000
Gross film rental (60%)	15,000,000
Less distribution fee (30%)	$ 4,500,000

Thus, the balance is $10,500,000. Superstar gets 10% of this amount, or $1,050,000. Now we have a balance of $9,450,000. From this balance we subtract distribution expenses, as in Example One, of $2,350,000. The net gross is now $7,100,000. The production, as before, cost $7 million. There is, therefore, a net profit of $100,000.

Star Number One gets 15% of $100,000	$15,000
Star Number Two gets 10% of $100,000	$10,000
Director receives 5% of $100,000	$ 5,000

The profit balance is now $70,000.

The writer receives 10%	$ 7,000
The producer receives 10%	$ 7,000

The net profit of the movie is therefore $56,000. This amount is divided among those who hold contingent points.

HYPOTHETICAL EXAMPLE THREE

In this case, Superstar receives 10 percent of the monies remaining after the distribution fee has been subtracted from the gross film rental. But the screenwriter receives 10 percent of the monies remaining after the cost of production has been deducted, but before the distributor receives reimbursement for actual expenses. Star One and Star Two then get their 15 percent and 10 percent respectively and the director gets 5 percent, the producer 10 percent. If anything is left as net net, the holders of contingency points get their share. Here's how a deal such as this would work out:

U.S. box-office gross	$25,000,000
Gross film rental (60%)	$15,000,000
Less distribution fee (30%)	$ 4,500,000

This leaves a balance of $10,500,000.

Superstar gets 10% of this amount	$1,050,000

Now, we are temporarily left with a balance of $9,450,000 from which we deduct the cost of production, $7 million, leaving a balance of $2,450,000.

The screenwriter gets 10% of this amount	$ 245,000
This leaves a balance of	$2,205,000

According to the contract, the distributor now recoups the actual cost of distribution expenses, $2,350,000. We can readily see, however, that there isn't enough money to pay this full amount. The distribution company therefore takes the $2,205,000 and has a loss on actual expenses of $145,000. No one else down the line gets a red dime because there is a loss on the movie. You might say that everyone else is grossed out!

Caution: do not take the above examples as gospel. They are offered as plausible possibilities. Going a step further, you should begin to make up your own set of variables, experiment with likely demands by cast and crew on big budget movies. Finally, each profit participant will be entitled to share in the profit, if any, as defined in each individual contract.

CHAPTER 10

DISTRIBUTORS AND EXHIBITORS: AN ONGOING RELATIONSHIP

Distributors deal with exhibitors on a daily basis, booking current films, leasing upcoming films, and announcing future releases. The three biggest box-office periods of the year are Christmas week, July 4th holiday week and Easter week. The entire summer is very lucrative playing time as well. The worst playing times are usually May and September, the changing seasons. Of course, these are generalizations and may vary from section to section of the country. Distributors maintain detailed records. They usually have daily overnight grosses of theaters in the leading 100 to 200 cities on their desks every morning. By keeping on top of every situation, getting a reading on which movies are and aren't doing business, distributors can make accurate decisions to increase or decrease advertising expenditures; for example, to try and get bigger and better grosses for their movies. It is not unusual for a distributor to guess within 5 percent of the ultimate gross of a movie based on the initial weekend grosses of opening engagements.

Home office executives are in constant contact with their branch office personnel. A movie is a very perishable commodity, and each one has to be handled with kid gloves. Some can be sold to the public through magazines—perhaps certain types of specialty magazines—with image-making catch phrases and with stars appearing for interviews after being carefully rehearsed on just what to say to lure the public into theaters. *The ballot boxes of the motion picture industry are the box offices.* The buck starts there! Everything is aimed at the patron. Critics don't pay to see movies. Distributors consider the patrons as the only legitimate critics, because they paid to see the movie and have a right to criticize. All the distributor wants to do is get the best terms from the most suitable theaters, get the movie played, see it gross well and get paid.

How does the distributor know he or she is getting the right count at the theater box offices? If he or she is in doubt, professional checkers will count the number of admissions in a theater. It is part of the cost of doing business, especially since this is a cash business.

OVERSEAS ("OFFSHORE") DISTRIBUTION

A typical commercial movie may bring in about 25 to 75 percent of its film rental from U. S. distribution. But there's a great big world out there—the overseas market. These are the usual primary markets:

Italy	Brazil
Australia	Mexico
Japan	Sweden
United Kingdom	Argentina
West Germany	Venezuela
France	Netherlands
Spain	Switzerland
South Africa	

Again, you are reminded that your movie should be suitable for worldwide distribution, to get the fullest return on its potential. A distributor can then develop multiple campaigns, individually crafted for disparate markets.

DISTRIBUTOR TALK

Distributors have their own jargon to describe the rest of the people in the film world. Sometimes it sounds like gibberish, but it isn't; it's just shop talk. Distributors know the truth about the marketplace and the people in it—the public and the tradepeople called exhibitors, producers and artists, moneymen and con men. Their speech is a running palaver about who is doing what to whom in the movie industry, and how they are doing it. Since the subject is money, their insights are full of pithy truths.

Of all the people in the movie industry, distributors as a group are the most colorful, yet they remain, in the public's eye, the most invisible, perhaps because they are the middle people, quite literally, between those who make movies and headlines and those who run the theaters and meet the public. The distributor is satisfied to get the show on the road so it can be seen and have a chance to make money.

Distributors generally know which producers are more likely to deliver movies that can be relied on to have the show-biz ingredients to make money. It is also the distributor's business to know who is paying bills and who isn't. Distributors can be quite charming, but all the while they are blueprinting new ways to secure greater returns for their one and only product—film.

BE YOUR OWN DISTRIBUTOR

Maybe you'd like to be your own distributor and not only produce your movie, but fashion its campaign as well. Even if you are versatile enough to do this sort of producer-distributor double-think routine, you will need lots of time and money to accomplish your goals. First you will have to decide when, where and how you will premiere your movie. Is it an action flim? Is it a war movie? Is it a sword and saddle epic? Is it a mystery or comedy or sex show? Is it a sci-fi or horror movie? Once you have the genre, you will have to go about researching what sort of campaign will get the movie off to a winning start. For example, where in the country is the best place to open it? This research requires a great deal of thought and study. Being your own distributor is a risky thing to predict, but let's give it a try and see what happens in a hypothetical example.

Let us suppose you have a movie that deals with a young congressman from Richmond, Virginia, who races stock cars and goes on to win local then regional championships. Then the congressman wins the state stock car racing title. There are great demands on him to enter the lucrative national contests. He faces a crisis; should he go on racing or continue in politics? It all comes to a head when he is offered the chance to run for the governorship of the state. He runs for governor, wins, than enters the national race and, while he doesn't win the top prize, he finishes in the top ten, proving he can succeed at both his profession and his hobby.

You have made this movie and either you don't want to let a distributor handle it, or they don't want it. In any event, you are going to distribute it yourself. Assume you've got $750,000 invested in production. You will need additional money to make prints and to advertise. You will also need to travel to contact theater bookers and buyers, the exhibitor organizations that lease movies to play in theaters. You will also need an office plus personnel, equipment and contract forms, among others. The amount of money you will need varies, as you will see later on.

Since the movie deals with a fictional racing-car politico from Virginia, suppose you decide to premiere it in the Washington, D.C. exchange territory. To determine how much you should spend on media advertising, handbills, giveaways, and area promotions, look at the Exchange City chart on pages 131-35. Here you note that on the average, the Washington, D.C. exchange provides about 3.6 percent of the North American film rentals. You should spend the same percentage of what you expect to earn nationally. The Washington, D.C. exchange covers the District of Columbia, the states of Virginia and Maryland, a small section of Delaware and a small part of West Virginia. Therefore, if you intend to premiere your film only in Virginia, then you will likely be aiming for only about one-quarter of that 3.6 percent—or 1 percent of all the money you garner in film rentals in the U.S. Suppose you perceive that the national film rental proceeds would come to about $2 million. Then, 1 percent of that amount would be $20,000. This figure may be revised as you will see later.

To determine how many prints you will need, look again at

your chart area. The key cities in Virginia are Newport News, Norfolk and Richmond. You also have other important markets in other cities:

Charlottesville	Blacksburg	Bassett
Danville	Salem	South Boston
Fredericksburg	Christiansburg	Martinsville
Lynchburg	Rocky Mount	Front Royal
Roanoke	Bedford	Pulaski
Staunton	Covington	Wytheville
Williamsburg	Clifton Forge	Galax
Winchester	Waynesboro	Radford
Portsmouth	Harrisonburg	Lexington
Suffolk	Culpepper	Buena Vista
Virginia Beach	Warrenton	Farmville
Petersburg	Manassas	Blackstone
	Quantico	

It will probably take fifty prints to cover these forty cities. You'll need the ten additional prints because in certain larger cities, including your three chart towns, you will be playing more than one theater.

The cost of these fifty prints is about $35,000. You will need to ship them and have them returned as well as provide coming attraction trailers, posters, and display material. Of course, you will use the prints and basic ad materials for later engagements, especially the key ad logo which is the design, copy and illustration that you'll be using in all your press material and ad campaigns.

Now let's examine those cities in Virginia you will likely want to get playdates in, all of them to open at the same time; it's called "day and date" in the movie industry.

To determine the best day and date on which to open your movie, consider two questions. What time of the year is it? What other movies are available for exhibitors to play? Remember that the best playtime is the summer; next is the Christmas/New Year's holiday period; then Easter and Memorial Day week. Since you have a racing movie and auto racing is on people's minds in May, especially with the Indianapolis 500 coming along on

Memorial Day weekend, if you are lucky you will secure playing time in fifty theaters the third week in May.

Will $20,000 be enough to spend to kick off your movie? You will likely spend more money, because you want to "buy a gross" (spend an inordinately large amount of money on advertising, to practically insure blockbuster grosses on your movie in the theaters). You will want to do great business so that the word will get around the country that your picture did, in fact, do great business, so that other exhibitors will want to play it. It's not unreasonable for you to figure a $40,000 campaign.

Why $40,000? Look back on your chart on page 135. Note that Washington, D.C., on average, accounts for 3.6 percent of the combined U.S. and Canadian gross. Now look at your total direct distribution costs. If you decide on $1 million, then the Washington, D.C. exchange should work out to 3.6 percent of that amount, or $36,000. Since this is the premiere of your movie, add another $4,000 in extra promotion. The money sure goes fast! But, you're looking to do at least 3.6 percent of your eventual U.S. and Canadian gross—perhaps more than that with a little extra promotion.

Now you can start adding up your costs:

Prints	$35,000	
Campaign	40,000	
Office Expenses		5,000 (est.)
Shipments		1,000 (est.)
Personnel		4,000 (est.)
Miscellaneous		5,000 (est.)
		$90,000

What will your movie have to gross in the fifty theaters for you to break even on the $90,000? Probably about $300,000. You are likely to get a gross film rental of 30 percent. Major companies would get 50 to 70 percent, but because you are independent the most you will get is 35 to 40 percent. Let us be safe, for the moment, and figure 30 percent. Thirty percent of $300,000 is $90,000; it will get you even in your premiere engagement. Now, how many people will have to see your movie to gross $300,000? If, admissions average around $2.50 per capita, it will take 120,000 Virginians to make $300,000. That means each theater must gross $6,000, attracting an average of 2,400 people each during the week, at an average admission price of $2.50 each. If you get lucky and your film does excellent box-office business, some exhibitors hold it over a second week. In this case you'll surely make a profit because only a very small ad campaign for the second week will be necessary; word of mouth will carry you along.

Suppose you gross $300,000 at the box office and you've played only fifty theaters, representing 1 percent of North American potential. If the rest of the country follows suit, your movie will gross $30 million. At 30 percent film rental, you'll collect $9 million.

The size of that last figure might suggest you would get back your production investment of $750,000. Remember, however, there are lots of exchange areas in the nation that don't give a hoot or holler about a Virginia politician or race car driver. You may never even get the first playdate on your film in those areas. It would, therefore, be wise of you to examine the exchange city possibilities. You may find that your film may only play in areas likely to accumulate only 50 percent of the potential revenue. If this is true, you will only collect half of that $9,000,000 or $4½ million rental. And, what about your campaign? It could cost you $2 million dollars to advertise your movie. While that's a lot of money, in terms of expenditures for movie advertising, it's less than average. For example, twenty national television spots could cost $2 million. Even if you gross $15 million at the box office and receive $4½ million in film rental, you'll have to subtract the cost of the movie ($750,000) and the cost of the campaign ($2 million) and more! You'll have to recoup the costs for shipping to about 2,500 theaters and back, and all your office costs including those hundreds of long-distance phone calls, staff, and travel. That is likely to come to another huge amount. What if some of your playdates run into bad weather or unexplained poor grosses? You may have looked like you are on your way to profits, but, unanticipated contingencies of all kinds could cut deeply into them. The point is that you are becoming aware of how detailed and chancy the business of distributing movies is.

EXHIBITION CONTRACT

What provisions does an exhibition contract (the licensing agreement between distributor and exhibitor) from a major company contain? They are fairly standard and usually have the following listed items:

Branch office
Date of contract
Salesperson
Contract number
Theater
Exhibitor's legal name
Location of the theater; city and state
Release number of the movie
Title of the Movie
Consecutive number of days and specific days of the week the movie will play
Minimum guaranteed film rental
Distributor's share of box-office receipts (in percentage terms)
Additional terms if any (There may be a provision that if the movie does a certain minimum at the box office it must be held over by the exhibitor at specified terms; also there may be special advertising provisions.)
Run (first run or second run.)
Clearance (clearance over other competing theaters in the area)
A page full of legalese, of actual interest to almost no one.

BOX-OFFICE STATEMENT:
EXHIBITOR REPORTS
WHAT THE MOVIE GROSSED

After the film has completed its run, the distributor sends the exhibitor a box-office statement with items to be filled out, including the gross of the movie. This form is completed by the exhibitor and returned to the distributor who, using the data, bills the exhibitor for the amount of film rental due and payable. Box-office statements are rather standard and generally include the following information:

Name of theater circuit
Name of theater
Town and state
Release number of movie to be exhibited
Title of movie
Playdate (exact dates picture will play)
Contract terms (see later discussion)
Second feature title, if any (there may be a second feature
    playing with your movie)
Provisions for each day's gross
An itemized and numbered accounting of tickets sold and
    prices of admission
Weekly gross
Authorized deductions (perhaps advertising costs) and/or
    cost of second feature, or house allowance (see
    discussion below, together with contract terms)
Total film rental due the distributor
Signature of the theater manager, circuit manager and,
    distributor's branch manager

FILM RENTAL TERMS

Film rental terms are a percentage of the difference between
box-office gross and house allowance (the amount of money it
costs the exhibitor to operate the theater weekly. This
percentage is paid by the exhibitor to the distributor.

Terms usually are 90%/10% over house allowance, with
basic minimums. That means 90% goes to the distributor and 10%
to the exhibitor after the house allowance has been deducted
from the box office gross. For example, the terms on a major
movie might be: $10,000 advance guarantee to the distributor
against four weeks guaranteed playing time, with a basic
minimum of 70 percent the first week, 60 percent the second
week, 50 percent the third week, and 40 percent the fourth week.

Exhibitors bid a cash guarantee because they are likely
asked to do so, together with competing exhibitors, by the
distributor.

Here is how the percentages work in practice. Let us say that
the house allowance comes to $3,000, and that the theater
grosses $10,000 that week:

Theater gross	$10,000
Less house allowance	$ 3,000
Balance	$ 7,000

The distributor gets 90 percent of the $7,000 or 70 percent of the $10,000, whichever is greater. Ninety percent of $7,000 is $6,300, 70 percent of $10,000 is $7,000, so the exhibitor must pay the distributor $7,000 in film rental. That leaves the exhibitor with zero profits from the box office that week. Of course, the exhibitor will be able to apply that $7,000 to the $10,000 advance guarantee, but it's still the same result in terms of dollars and cents.

The second week of the engagement is likely to produce a smaller gross at the theater box office. For example:

Second week theater gross	$7,000
Less house expense	$3,000
Balance	$4,000

The distributor this week will get 90 percent of $4,000 or 60 percent of $7,000, whichever is higher. Since 90 percent of $4,000 is $3,600 and 60 percent of $7,000 is $4,200, the exhibitor will have to pay the distributor the higher amount and, on paper, lose $200 that week. Later on, under the section on Exhibition, you will see how the exhibitor copes with this situation.

There are movies with lesser potential that have lower terms. In addition, by the time that movies get to theaters in smaller towns and later runs, the terms decrease. On an average, exhibitors pay about forty to fifty cents on every dollar they take in at the box office to distributors as film rental.

When you read or hear publicity gossip that a movie grossed twenty million dollars, remember that's the figure for what the movie grossed at the theater box offices. The gross film rental is considerably less, probably around 45% of the box-office gross.

Besides percentage term arrangements, there are some urban repertory as well as small-town theaters that lease movies on a flat-rental basis. That means, they pay a stipulated cash price—$25 to $500 or more—for the rental of a movie. Therefore, the distributor really doesn't know just what the gross is of those movies, because without a percentage rental there's no need for a box-office statement. In view of flat-rentals, you can readily see that it's almost impossible to arrive at a precise amount of money that most movies gross in America. Except for movies leased solely on percentage rentals, it is impossible to secure exact figures on the exact box-office gross of any film.

To complicate matters further, there are exchanges in the country called "double-feature" territories while other exchanges are referred to as "single-feature" territories. A double-feature territory is one in which most theaters play two movies, a "double-bill." Sometimes both movies are from the same distributor, sometimes they're not. Even if they're from the same distributor, it's more than likely that there are two different producers involved and, two different financial arrangements between the producers and distributor. One of the two features may receive a healthy percentage of the theater grosses while the other is sold for a low flat-rental.

You should be aware of all these different types of rental arrangements if and when you enter into a contract with a distribution company. You will probably have to allow the distributor the opportunity to lease your movie at flat-rentals after the initial distribution on percentage terms. Because of these complications it will be necessary for you to negotiate with the aid of your attorney. You want the best possible arrangements so that your movie has a chance to garner the greatest rentals on percentage leases.

REVIEWS AND ALTERATIONS
OF CONTRACT TERMS

Exhibitors generally complain that they are paying film rentals so high that they can't make a profit. Sometimes, on the other hand, a movie disappoints by not living up to its potential and does poorly at the box office. In cases like these, the exhibitor will ask the distributor to review—that is, reduce—the original terms. Asking the distributor for a reduction in terms is very common and has been a long-time industry practice. Many distributors will tell the exhibitor that after the engagement, if the gross is disappointing, they will "look" or give a second "wink" or "blink" at the terms and reduce them a little; that usually means reducing the original terms by about ten to twenty-five percent. This calls for an alteration of the contract based on comparisons of previous grosses on similar movies in the recent past. In the movie business, everyone keeps detailed records. Precedents are essential.

Suppose you played a gangster movie from the same company at 50% and grossed $5,000. Let's say you asked for a reduction in terms. The distributor would look up his records and might find that you usually gross $7,000 on comparable gangster movies and, when you do, you pay 50 percent, but when you gross only $5,000 they have in the past altered the original contract from 50 percent to 37½ percent. In such cases, they are likely to make the same reductions again. No matter how much distributors deny it, they usually know the gross of everyone else's movies in every theater because they historically share such information. Therefore, they have some excellent records of just what any particular theater grosses. They will even have a record of every day's weather and of any extenuating circumstances, such as a local parade or holiday or anything else that may account for an otherwise unexplained increase or decrease in gross.

The real recordkeepers of the industry are the distributors They know everyone's business—theirs, the producer's and the exhibitor's. Distributors deal in truths, not legends or facts. The distributor's world for many in the industry has traditionally been a closed one and I hope I've opened it up for you.

PART 4

EXHIBITION

CHAPTER 11

RETAILING MOVIES

Movies are made to be retailed. Movie retailers are known as exhibitors. They are in a cash business called exhibition. Exhibitors show commercial motion pictures in single-purpose structures commonly known as theaters. Customers pay an admission charge to see a motion picture in a theater. Theaters are also popularly called cinemas. There is a growing trend in America, namely multiple-screen theaters. A multiple-screen theater houses more than one auditorium and, therefore, more than one film screen. Later on in this section we will discuss the reasons for the growing popularity of multiple-screen theaters, but for the moment it's important to note that people in the industry generally refer to theaters as screens. Just as cinema is a synonym for theater, auditorium is a synonym for screen.

There are about 16,500 screens in the United States. No one seems to know exactly how many because old and new ones close and open for business daily. But, at any given moment, at least one of each of the following kinds of theaters are open for business in America:

Single Screen Theater: One screen (auditorium)
Twin: Two screens
Triple: Three screens
Quad: Four screens
Fiveplex: Five screens
Sixplex: Six screens
Sevenplex: Seven screens
Eightplex: Eight screens
Nineplex: Nine screens
Tenplex: Ten screens

Exhibitors are theater owners or lessees of theaters. Many owners operate their own theaters. They maintain direct control over theater operations and the contracting for and booking of movies. In industry terms, they buy (lease) and book (date) commercial motion pictures from distributors for their theaters.

On the other hand, some owners defer the buying and booking of movies to agents. In so doing, the theater owner becomes part of an organization devoted solely to negotiating, contracting for, securing prints of desired movies and, perhaps, settling (reducing) film rental terms on films that don't gross up to expectations. The agency, acting in behalf of a number of independent theater owners, also offers its clients insights about the potential value of movies.

The buyers and bookers talk about available and future movie releases each working day—among themselves, with distribution executives, and with other buyers and bookers in other exchange areas in the country. They are constantly trading information, rumors, theater grosses, hoping to sort it all out and make sense of the grossing potentials of current and soon-to-be-released motion pictures. The agents then buy and book, usually with the advice and consent of each of their clients, after informing them about the market and current releases.

THEATER CIRCUITS

In addition to individuals or companies owning one theater, there are companies owning or controlling more than one theater—in other words, a theater circuit. Here is a listing of six of the largest circuits in the United States:

1. General Cinema Corp.	About 800 screens
2. United Artists Theaters	About 600 screens
3. William Forman's theater interests, including RKO-Stanley Warner, Pacific Theaters and Cinema 5	About 400 screens
4. American Multi Cinema	About 350 screens
5. Commonwealth Theaters	About 350 screens
6. Plitt Theaters, including ABC Theaters	About 300 screens

The larger theater circuits usually maintain three in-house departments to manage their business:

Theater Operations: This department deals with scouting future theater locations, theater designs, construction, property maintenance, community relations, personnel salaries, supplies, utilities, insurances, taxes, repairs, telephone, and rent.

Buying & Booking: Once a movie is contracted for by the buyer, the booker arranges for a print of the movie to play; this means a 'playdate' for the movie, usually set by the distributor.

Advertising: Depending upon the size of the operation, film advertising, which is set by the distributor, is brought to the attention of exhibitor's buying and booking department or, a separate department. If it is a separate advertising department, it is likely to be in constant contact with advertising people in distributor home offices, talking about details of the campaign budgets, publicity and promotion.

CHARTING GROSSES

It is a reasonable estimate that theaters in chart towns account for about 60 to 80 percent of all North American film rentals on movies with broad commercial appeal. As for art films, most foreign films, filmed concerts, ballet and opera, a greater percentage of film rentals is derived from exhibition in college town theaters.

EXHIBITION AND THE INDEPENDENT PRODUCER-DISTRIBUTOR

If you as an independent producer want to consider distributing your movie independently, you can, in theory, reach a potential market of about 3,000 playdates with only about fifty to 100 calls. The reason is simple: just select the fifty to 100 largest booking and buying agencies and theater circuits and offer them your film. If they accepted your offer, you probably would account for at least 50 percent of all the money you might expect in the way of film rentals from a thorough and complete distribution. Of course, it's costly to travel the country and maintain personnel and follow-up for collections, but in theory it can be done.

It may not be practical, however. For example, suppose your movie has the potential to do good business in small towns and rural areas? If so, you need a professional distribution organization to reach the owners, agents and circuits of theaters in remote areas. There are movies that yield their greatest returns from the heartland of America, the South, Southwest and Midwest; they may not even play in New York or Los Angeles. Even if they do, you're likely to get greater net film rentals from small-town theaters for at least two reasons. One, the story may be more appealing to people in small towns. Two, it costs much less to put on a first-class local ad campaign in a small town. You will always be dealing in judgment calls, and that always means you are putting your money where you think it will garner the greatest rate of return.

EXHIBITION: WHAT DOES IT COST TO OPEN YOUR DOORS EVERY WEEK?

What does it cost to run a theater, exclusive of film rental costs? Or, as they say in the trade, "What does it cost to open your doors every week?" Here are five examples of weekly costs rounded off to the nearest even figures, based on actual records of operating theaters:

	Theater A	Theater B	Theater C	Theater D	Theater E
Rent	496	648	520	1040	2516
Salaries	1412	1363	1531	1514	1762
General & administrative	730	995	1194	913	812
Advertising	175	180	190	180	358
Depreciation	10	18	54	63	587
Insurance	21	25	28	26	101
Taxes	238	257	253	348	106
Repairs & maintenance	73	56	189	173	216
Telephone	11	15	11	20	62
Theater supplies	73	56	139	173	87
Utilities	165	316	312	410	331
Miscellaneous	96	171	129	140	562
Total Weekly Expenses exclusive of film rental costs	3500	4100	4500	5000	7500

MULTIPLE SCREENS

There are many advantages to multiple screens. If you had a quad—four screens in one theater—you probably could save money by having only one manager instead of four, resulting in economy of operation. In addition, you would have a single projection booth, therefore a single projectionist instead of four projectionists. If two of the four movies were lousy and two were box-office hits, then the two poor grossers would benefit. Why? Because patrons who couldn't get into the two filled auditoriums might very well see one of the other two movies simply because they made the trip, were there, and it was too late to go elsewhere to see a movie. Furthermore, if you had a real box-office smash and you had a quad, then you could book it into all four auditoriums and have a show starting every twenty-five or thirty minutes! Another reason for multiple screens is that it allows the theater owner to book movies for different interests. For example, the exhibitor could book a western, a sci-fi, love story and mystery, one in each auditorium. In that way, he or she would be catering to the broadest public tastes every day of every week.

Years ago exhibitors had a general reputation as showpeople; today they are businesspeople. No longer are they building palaces; today they are building auditoriums. And, why not? Kids who go to the movies nowadays were brought up on television. They watched a 12-inch screen in their 10′ by 12′ bedrooms. Small-theater auditoriums with small screens just happen to have similar boundaries, relatively speaking. So, the kids can go to the movies and, psychologically, feel right at home. Multiscreen theaters should continue to grow in popularity for all the above reasons.

EXHIBITION: LEASING A MOVIE

How does a theater go about leasing a movie? Distributors solicit exhibitors, usually with bid letters, inviting them to bid against their competitors. There are two kinds of bid letters:

Blind Bid. In this case the exhibitor doesn't get a chance to see the movie in question prior to submitting a bid for it. Therefore, the exhibitor is bidding blindly. Actually, the bid is blind only in the sense that the exhibitor doesn't see the film; the exhibitor is, on the other hand, given the facts about the movie: who's in it, who directed it, who produced it, who is distributing it, plus the kind of advertising campaign and dollar expenditures allocated to promote it. Those who are against blind bidding argue that, while seeing or not seeing a movie prior to bidding for it doesn't necessarily make it easier to pick a potential winner from loser, seeing a movie does help the exhibitor to spot a "dog"—a highly ballyhooed movie that doesn't do business— thereby avoiding a high cash bid based on high expectations. The exhibitor would like to see every movie prior to laying out hard cash guarantees, but this isn't always possible.

For example, a distributor may send out a bid letter in January offering exhibitors a movie for July release. Likely as not, the movie is in postproduction and won't be completed until July or late June. The exhibitor must set July 4th bookings far in advance, because it is an excellent play time. If he or she doesn't bid for the movie in January, his or her summer playtime could be ruined because, most likely all the other distributors are asking for January bids on July releases. If exhibitors know that they have the movie for July, they can start ballyhooing it, running coming attraction trailers in May, building up a potential audience. On the other hand, the distributor might say that if the exhibitors want to know if they have a potentially big grossing summer movie, they must join the distributor in waiting on the production team to complete the film; they must join in taking the risk that the movie may be a hit or a bomb.

As an independent, the only time you may become involved in having your movie blind bid is if it's distributed by a major company.

Non-Blind Bid. In this case the exhibitor sees the movie before submitting a bid. Even then, it's hard to guess the grossing potential of a film. An example of a movie that exhibitors saw prior to bids and which, as a group, thought wouldn't do much business, was *Star Wars*. This example alone ought to point out how hard it is to pick out a winner, even after it is completed and backed by a massive publicity campaign.

On the other hand, there are movies that, as they say in the trade, "everybody buys except the public." This would include all those movies that critics rave about, exhibitors, distributors and producers love for its grossing potential, but patrons just don't support in accordance with their expectations. An example would be *Nashville.*

HOUSE NUTS

A theater's weekly expense is generally referred to as the house overhead, house nut, or house expense. In plain terms it's what it costs you, as an exhibitor, to open your doors for business weekly. This figure becomes the house allowance on film rentals. For example, on page 205 we listed five different house expenses. Let's use the smallest one—$3,500—as an example. The exhibitor contracts to play a movie with terms of 90/10 over 70%:

Box-office gross for the week $10,000
Less house allowance recouped by exhibitor   3,500

                                                               $ 6,500
90% of $6,500 to distributor $ 5,850
10% retained by exhibitor $ 650

However, there is a floor (minimum) of 70 percent on this deal. As previously mentioned, this means that the exhibitor must pay whichever is greater: 90 percent of gross after deduction for house allowance or 70 percent of gross.

Seventy percent of $10,000 is $7,000, which is greater than the $5,850 rental based on 90 percent/10 percent. Therefore, the exhibitor must remit $7,000 to the distributor and retain $3,000. Since it costs $3,500 weekly to run this theater, the exhibitor lost $500 on the box-office gross for that period. The exhibitor can make this up, however, primarily through concession sales. Concession sales usually come to 15 to 25 percent of the box-office receipts, on average. For example:

Box-office gross for week $10,000
Concession sales for week (20%)   2,000

How much profit is there in concessions? It depends on whether the exhibitor runs his own concession or leases it out to a professional dealer. On average, the net profit is likely to range around 25 percent. In the above example the exhibitor, by netting $500 profit on concession sales, breaks even for the week.

MORE MONEY

There are other ways for exhibitors to try to make a profit. For example, during the morning hours, they may lease their theaters to fund-raising organizations, church groups, for corporate seminars or sales meetings, and other activities. On weekends they sometimes book local or area musical groups for midnight shows. They also book special Saturday and holiday matinees for young children. Remember, the musical groups and film matinees attract young people who account for the greatest per capita sales at concession stands. Teenagers get hungry at midnight and youngsters are always ready for sweets. Many times they will pay as much for candy as they did for admission to the theater.

As it is, a good guess is that most theaters exhibiting current movies with broad commercial appeal average 1½ to 3½ percent net profit on their combined annual box office and concession grosses. That means that a theater grossing a combined $400,000 would net between $6,000 and $14,000 a year. Don't forget that those are net profit figures, after all overhead, including salaries, have been paid.

BIG SPENDERS

It should be obvious that theater owners want movies that attract the most people because the bigger the audience the bigger the concession sales. This is true for general run movies, especially films that attract very young audiences. On the other hand, "arty" movies have traditionally generated smaller concession sales. For example, a Disney movie could account for candy and soda pop sales of around 70 percent of admission prices; if a child paid an admission price of $2, he or she might buy $1.40 worth of candy. On the other hand, 'arty' films usually attract older audiences or, if they aren't older, people who just want to get wrapped up in the movie, not a candy bar. They might pay an adult price of around $3.50 but only spend 5 percent, or 17½ cents per capita, on concession items. The pressure to book commercial movies with popular appeal—sometimes at any price, any film rental—becomes apparent as a way of life for exhibitors. Many of them, unhappily, realize that they are more in the concession business than the movie business—that they need big grossing movies to bring in big spending food customers.

CHAPTER 12

RELEASING A MOVIE TO EXHIBITORS

Distributors usually release movies to exhibitors in one of five ways: general release, saturation, geographic, selective, and exclusive.

General release: The movie is available to most first-run chart-town theaters across the country.

Saturation: The movie is available not only to first-run chart towns but also to towns nearby those chart cities. It is a broader release than a general release.

Geographic: The movie is available only in a certain defined region of the country; for example, the South, which would include the Charlotte, Atlanta and Jacksonville exchanges. By releasing a movie in "waves" (geographically) prints can also be shipped in waves, resulting in great savings.

Selective: The movie is available only in a small number of theaters in each exchange territory, hoping to build word of mouth (WOM) and have a later saturation release.

Exclusive: The movie is available only in a single theater in each chart town, in hopes of building an image for the movie as an important and exclusive entertainment, later to be followed by selective and saturation bookings.

A TRIO OF GUESSTIMATES

A trio of "guesstimates" would be that about twenty to twenty-five million people pass through theater box offices weekly in America at an average admission price of about $2.50, accounting for an amount approaching $3 billion a year at the box offices.

As an aggregate, exhibition is big business; all big businesses have charts like the one in the following section.

FILM RENTAL TERMS

Let's go back to the example of the theater with the $3,500 weekly overhead. On a 90/10 deal with no minimum percent, here is a formula for figuring what the exhibitor will pay in film rental to the distributor:

Where picture grosses the following number, multiplied by weekly house expense	The distributor will receive the equivalent of the following percentages of the box-office gross from the exhibitor
8.00	78.75%
7.00	77.7
6.00	75.0
5.00	72.0
4.75	71.1
4.50	70.0
4.25	68.8
4.00	67.5
3.75	66.0
3.60	65.0
3.50	64.3
3.33	63.0
3.25	62.3
3.00	60.0

Where picture grosses the following number, multiplied by weekly house expense	The distributor will receive the equivalent of the following percentages of the box-office gross from the exhibitor
2.75	57.3
2.50	54.0
2.25	50.0
2.00	45.0
1.80	40.0
1.75	38.5
1.50	30.0
1.25	18.0
1.25	10.0
1.00	No film rental

Using the above table for a movie that grosses eight times the house expense of a theater with a $3,500 weekly overhead, here's how it looks:

Box-office gross (8 times $3,500)	$28,000
Less exhibitor recoupment of house nut	3,500
	$24,500

Ninety percent of $24,500 equals $22,050 which is the same as 78.75 percent of the $28,000 gross. The chart works!

SLIDING SCALES

There are other ways of arriving at film rentals. In the past and even today in small towns, exhibitors have sliding scales that provide formulas for paying anywhere from 25 to 60 percent for film rental. These methods of arriving at film rentals were the basis for the business years ago and a foundation on which almost all current film rentals are based.

First, the seven-day week was (in some cases still is) divided up into units, depending on traditional grossing capacities of various days of the week, as follows:

Sunday	1 or 2 units
Monday	1 unit
Tuesday	1 unit
Wednesday	1 unit
Thursday	1 unit
Friday	2 units
Saturday	2 or 3 units

So, if a movie played Friday through Sunday, just three days, it would be six units of playing time. If a film played a theater Wednesday through Saturday, it would mean it got either six or seven units of playing time, depending on how you arrived at your 100 percent figure. It is clear that weekend business is usually considered to be the best playing time in most commercial theaters. Playing a movie on Friday and Saturday alone usually means getting 40 to 50 percent of the week's business.

THE 33.33% SCALE: EXAMPLE ONE

One scale allows an exhibitor to earn 33.33 percent of the amount he or she pays in film rental. For example, in the theater with $3,500 overhead, during the seven days of the week the exhibitor offers ten units of play time. A unit is equal to $3,500 divided by 10. In the following scale, the exhibitor pays between 25 and 60 percent film rental, depending on the gross, but at all times earns 33.33 percent profit.

25%	1.454 times $350 per unit (expense p.u.)
27.5%	1.539 times $350 per unit
30%	1.639 times $350 per unit
32.5%	1.756 times $350 per unit
35%	1.875 times $350 per unit
37.5%	2.000 times $350 per unit
40.0%	2.142 times $350 per unit

42.5%   2.307 times $350 per unit
45.0%   2.500 times $350 per unit
47.5%   2.727 times $350 per unit
50.0%   3.000 times $350 per unit
52.5%   3.333 times $350 per unit
55.0%   3.747 times $350 per unit
57.5%   4.283 times $350 per unit
60.0%   5.000 times $350 per unit

Suppose this theater plays a movie for one week and grosses five times its house net, $17,500. According to the chart the theater should pay 60 percent film rental, because the movie earned that much on the sliding scale, the exhibitor should be left with a 33.33 percent profit.

Gross	$17,500
Less 60% film rental	10,500
Balance	$ 7,000

It costs the exhibitor $3,500 to run the theater, so he's left with a $3,500 profit. That's 33.33 percent of the amount the distributor gets as film rental—$10,500. The scale works!

INDEPENDENT GUESSING

Of the approximately 16,500 screens in America, grossing an aggregate approaching $3 billion, my guess is that about 30 percent of the screens gross 70 percent of the dollars. Converting percentages to numbers, approximately 4,950 screens gross nearly $2 billion annually; approximately 11,550 screens gross less than $1 billion annually.

Therefore, if my assumption is correct, 70 percent of the screens each gross less than $100,000 annually, exclusive of concession sales. That isn't much. It's very likely that many of these businesses are run as "mom and pop" family operations, or, if some of these screens are part of large theater circuits, they may very well be operating on marginal profits or losses. It would be reasonable to assume that many of these low-grossing auditoriums may shut down in the near future, unless perhaps they can lease movies at terms of less than 90/10 with minimums of 70 and 60 percent.

The effort to eke out a profit from marginal theaters should be of special interest to independent producer-distributors. Why? The low-to-medium-budget movie will probably find a market in smaller theaters; the independent movie will likely carry lower film rental terms, be available immediately and have the extra push that independents usually try for in local campaigning, especially in small-town newspapers.

On the other hand, if you have ambitions about becoming an independent exhibitor, it's likely as not that you'll start small, with a single theater, and try to improve its grossing capacities and profit-making. If so, the sliding scales in this section should be of particular interest to you. They are meant to inform you about the dollars and cents of film rentals—the point of departure between a small profit or small loss in many small-grossing theaters.

SCRIPT TO CINEMA

There are "haves" and "have-nots"—"insiders" and "non-insiders"—in exhibition, as there are in production and distribution. Independent producers, distributors and exhibitors are, frankly, have-nots and non-insiders trying to either get into the business or, if in it, struggling to survive. Why? Well, let's answer the question with a questionable prediction. In the near future it's possible that the ten largest production-distribution companies could sit down with the ten largest theater circuits and booking and buying agencies, and wrap up most of the potential film rentals in America.

Where does that leave the independents? Probably grim but hopeful, as always, that somehow, somewhere, some way they will find their place in the movie world, at whatever the cost. Why should any reasonable independent expect it to be different? Movie production, distribution and exhibition is really big business. I'd guess there's at least a combined $5 billion investment in the real estate and equipment we call theaters in America. They need an orderly flow of movies backed by large marketing budgets, in volume, at film rental terms they can live with.

Theaters are film guzzlers; they get just so many days of playing time out of each movie. Unlike automobiles, there's no EPA mileage estimate to each movie; there's almost no way of predicting how long each film will play in any given theater. The motion picture industry, from script to cinema, is a dicey adventure.

A concluding note for those of you who may be considering a career in exhibition: I suggest that you spend as much time as possible studying the field of retailing. Many colleges have retailing majors where you can study marketing, accounting, promotion and publicity. In addition, consider a summer job as a theater usher, another one as a clerk in a theater circuit office, another as an intern in a booking and buying agency—all of these on-location jobs should help you make up your own mind if you sincerely want a career in exhibition.

Where can you find these jobs? By taking the initiative and applying for work at a theater near you. Speak to the theater manager about summer or weekend employment. In my experience, people who are willing to take this single step forward have a better than average chance of landing a job and an opportunity to test their interest in a career.

A word of caution: Many movie fans have ambitions of having their own theaters. That's fine and dandy, but owning and running a theater is a day-to-day business—a hard one at that—and not a hobby. If you're a movie buff and want your own theater, it might be cheaper to build a screening room in your basement or garage. Buying or leasing a real theater means you are making an expensive long-term business commitment. For most business people, the worst horror in the world is not making a profit. Be aware that, in exhibition, it's easier to lose money than make money. That's because most movies aren't big box-office hits, and even if they are, their film rental terms are very high. Exhibition is a retailing business. Unlike many other retailing businesses, it's got some glamour because you're selling movie stars and dreams. Still, it's a business, with payrolls, taxes, insurance bills and long hours.

See you at the movies. Whatever path you chose "may the force be with you."

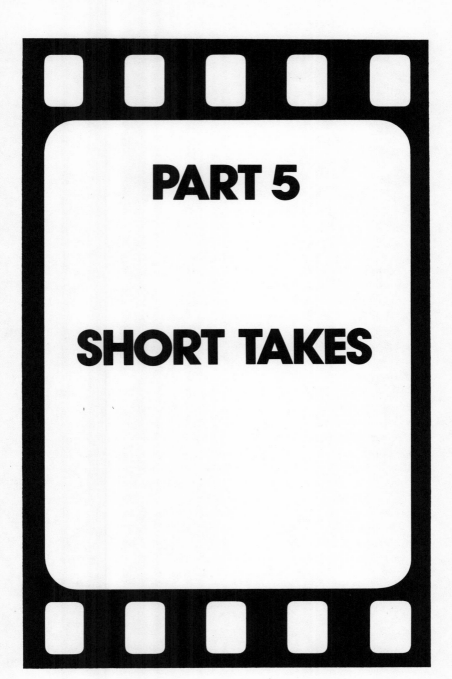

PART 5

SHORT TAKES

FALLY MARCUS

Fally Marcus is a term I'd like not to see lost in history. Its roots are in vaudeville but it applies to movie theaters—at least some theaters, the ones that are "test engagements." That means your movie is finished and you want to test it in small theaters in small towns, so the press won't take notice. Here you can experiment with last-minute editing or cuts before you formalize the movie and the campaign for national distribution in first-run theaters in major cities.

You test your movie in Fally Marcuses.

INOFFENSIVE MOVIES

I was once assigned the task of visiting as many of the theaters in America as was possible, to book playdates for movies. I also had to visit vacation resorts of all kinds, country clubs, cloistered convents, prisons and asylums. Everybody wanted movies, but they all wanted or needed different kinds of movies for their specialized clientele. Prisons particularly wanted inoffensive movies. I remember being in offices with convicted murderers and discussing the *inoffensive* movies I had in my trunk for the inmates. I was cautioned by prison authorities never to sell them a flick they might throw a shoe at and thereby ruin the screen. I remember, however, noticing many torn, ripped, taped, and sewn screens in these places.

I was usually their only human touch with Hollywood and show biz. They'd greet me, yell, cheer and stomp their feet when I unraveled the advertising material I'd brought. They sure appreciated the fantasy world of those colorful publicity packages, but it was a little sad, even if I left with a pocketful of playdates on my movies, to see all those arms waving through the barred windows, yelling; the sounds stayed with me a long time. Till now, I guess.

DATA

Some individuals and research firms chart movies like the weather. They design a synoptic movie chart with conventional symbols and shadings, plot observations from various points, and compile data for analysis. The charts are all very academic, rational, and helpful. Yet, it remains for experienced industry personnel to coordinate, collate and interpret the data, which, like the weather, can change from hour to hour. Sometimes, long-range predictions can be made with assurance, for the times are always changing. If western, musical, comedy, or gangster genres are out of vogue, then my suggestion is to write scripts in those genres. There is a rhythm to it all. The script you write this year is really prepped to be a movie several years from now, so it's wise to track trends over five- and ten-year periods. It may help you to write a script that will be among the first considered when a new trend is "discovered"—that is when Hollywood decides to rejuvenate a species or class of films.

SEEING ISN'T NECESSARILY BELIEVING

It should be pointed out that sometimes the persons who receive credits on the screen didn't actually do the assigned job. Many writers do not take or get credit. Other credits may be sold for cash. The buyer, having nothing to do with the actual performance of the assigned credit, may have bought it for his or her résumé, to have a credential for future work. It's an investment in the future, or at least one hopes so. Of course, if the film is a commercial success the buyer can take the credit and make something of it.

CRITICS

The word "critic," to me, has a negative connotation. I prefer the us of the term "reviewer." A good reviewer formalizes his or her many impressions into a total statement, intended for a movie audience. The reviewer is not writing for the general public. The movie audience is narrower and identifiable. The first job of a reviewer is either to advise the audience to see the movie and tell why, or to advise them not to see the movie, and tell why. For me, the best kind of reviewers have an audience's response to a film—the kind of response that communicates perceptions and feelings clearly, formally, completely. My favorite reviewers write as if they were discussing the movie with a group of movie fans, interested in all aspects of the film.

MOVIE BUFFS

Movie buffs usually see just about every sci-fi flick, and most of the horror genre, too. They are attracted to the fanciful, freakish, inconceivable and bizarre. Since nearly all sci-fi movies concern themselves with individuals struggling to be individuals in a world of increasing state controls, I assume that reveals something about movie buffs—that they are very concerned about maintaining personal freedoms and self-sufficiency in the face of increasing governmental restraints and restrictions.

As for their interest in horror movies, this category is concerned with illusion, escapism, imagination, and however fanciful, the forces of Good versus the forces of Evil. Usually, Evil wins the early skirmishes, but Good triumphs in the end. The resolution of the movie may leave the issue in doubt, creating a *faux air*, perhaps to be resolved by a sequel. The ongoing thread, therefore, is imagination, even after the movie has ended.

TALK TO EXHIBITORS

If you relate to things in terms of glittering generalities, then

Production is where the glory is;
Distribution is where the power is; and
Exhibition is where the money is.

An exhibitor is in a cash business, retailing movies. Many exhibitors are in other cash businesses as well—restaurants, real estate, motels, bars and grills, and bowling alleys. They don't see themselves as museum curators exhibiting art on their walls, but rather as storekeepers, exhibiting commercial movies on their screens. They are interested in paying customers, not deficit funding of works of art. Anyone who contemplates making a commercial movie should spend hours with exhibitors, especially the ones under the gun, the ones with theaters that need a new, first-run product every week to stay alive and turn a profit. I recommend it as a learning experience. The exhibitors are the ones in daily contact with the public. If you want to produce a movie for public consumption, the quickest way to understand what the public is all about is to interview exhibitors in-depth. They want movies which will do business. Heed their advice and profit from it.

WRITING RITUALS

Writers have rituals. Some like to type, others work in longhand with pen or pencil or crayon; many work on yellow-lined paper, or scraps of paper or restaurant napkins. Some dictate into a machine and play it back for corrections and rewrites. It's all very mysterious. And, advancing to content, some only feel comfortable if they know the ending right from the start of their writing. Others begin without knowing the ending or resolution. Still others work at defining their characters, writing biographies of them, then once they have pictures in their head of what their characters "look like," they write a story about them.

Whatever the style, long after the story and characters are forgotten, the writer's point of view, the writer's perception and comment on a slice of life, the writer's *theme*, woven into the transferring of a creatively imagined touch of reality, not an artistically rendered movie visual, is what remains discussed. Critics and reviewers jaw about what the movie had to *say* and how close to the truth it is in reflecting contemporary society.

MISE-EN-SCÈNE

I recommend that aspiring screenwriters take acting and directing classes. They should experience first-hand just what happens to scripts after they leave the writer's desk and make their way to other professionals. They should gain greater insights into their own work and, at the same time, improve and enrich their understanding of the mise-en-scène.

LOOKING, LEARNING, AND DOING

Everyone talks about movies, but hardly anyone writes them. Instead of thinking and talking about what you want to do, start doing it! Most people lead boring lives, so aim to give them escapist entertainment. Don't talk down to your audiences. Just talk to them. If you write comedy or horror stuff the worst thing that can happen to you is to have audiences laugh *at* the movie instead of laughing *with* the movie. You can make the theatricality of 98% of your script work if you pay hard and fast attention to giving the audience a solid 2% truth. For example, if you're writing a horror or sci-fi movie, the audience knows it's in for a fantasy ride. Why not surprise them by starting it off with a common occurence, like driving down a typical road in a typical car on a typical day when something atypical happens, as it could happen to anyone at anytime in the normal course of life. You're neither being contentious nor eristic, but rather logically didactic, and plausible, to boot. You are drawing your willing audience into a reasonable situation, and then springing your figurative imagination on them with a hearty rendering of escapist entertainment. It's your job.

AGENCY FORM

If you have a completed screenplay and wish to submit it to an agent, you will be given a form to fill out. It usually has the following:

1. Title of screenplay
2. The leading characters in the screenplay
3. A brief—about twenty-five words—summary of the story
4. A brief—about fifteen words—summary of the theme
5. Length of screenplay; exact number of pages and approximate number of words
6. Who owns the screenplay and has full rights to it
7. You will have to sign and have the form notarized.

THE MID-NINETEENTH CENTURY AND THE MOVIES

Mid- and late-nineteenth-century romanticism in America meant thousands of short stories and hundreds of magazines dealing with the following:

- New experiences
- Desire for originality and innovation
- Intensity of expression
- Superstitions, folklore, occult and legends
- High adventure on the open plains
- Glossy truth, idealized truth, but not the real truth
- Unlocking the yearnings of the human race
- Vivid, graphic, expressive and vibrant word sketches, pictures, scenes and landscapes
- An enthusiasm for life and a willingness to become involved with the sensational aspects of life through the mind and eyes of another person
- A sense of urgency and immediacy
- The life styles of other people
- An active interest in unique characters and events
- Light entertainment as well as an interest in the mystical, mysterious, and exotic
- The pursuit of sensationalism, not personally, but as something to be read and enjoyed
- Romantic wonderment
- Interest in the newest, most modern, unusual, uncommon, original, esoteric novelties
- Moral lessons to be learned from life

- The illusion of lifelike experiences
- Imaginative expression, bountiful color and powerful stories
- Faraway, rich and florid places

Do you think this list reads a little like some of the roots of movie subjects and themes these past eighty years? Certainly enough to make the comparison between what movies deal with and with what romantic revivalism in America dealt with, remembering that the American movement had its roots in European writings.

GET INVOLVED

If you are interested in a career in distribution, contact all the major film companies. Off and on, willy-nilly, some producing-distributing firms have training programs open to men and women. If you're hired you will likely be trained in some branch office in an exchange city. You'll be doing office and booking chores for about six to eight months at a very nominal salary. If you survive, you will be promoted to a sales position in another branch office, somewhere else in America. If you survive that experience, you'll likely be promoted to a branch sales manager or even branch manager. Be prepared to move and take every opportunity offered to you. The possibility always exists that if you refuse an offer your future with the company may be stopped.

Hardly anyone knows about careers in distribution, especially so on campuses, where students are busy expressing themselves about how they plan to write, direct and produce meaningful movies like Truffaut (who never made an American movie, probably because American film companies see him as a guy you arrange a free lunch for at a museum rather than someone to make a movie that will make money in major American theaters, where people have to pay to get in). Eventually, all those "artists" will, of necessity, have to go to distributors to learn the facts of movie life—not the "facts" in the gassy gossip columns with their planted publicity pieces, but instead the real truth about movies, as it appears in excruciatingly detailed contracts followed by real checks for real money.

If you get an interview with an American distribution company don't tell them all about the latest out-of-focus foreign film with "writin' on the bottom" (subtitles!) that you saw and just adored. Forget it, or they'll forget you. Instead, discuss the number of shipments, ad campaigns, film rentals, distribution patterns and the release calendar of the company. They'll know you mean business and that you want to get involved.

MOVIE RATINGS

The Motion Picture Association of America rating system for commercial movies is as follows:

G — General audiences; all ages admitted
PG— Parental Guidance suggested; some material may not be suitable for pre-teenagers
R — Restricted; under 17 (or 16, depending on your area) requires accompanying parent or adult guardian
X — No one under 17 admitted

If you don't submit your movie to the MPAA for rating, then regardless of its content, it becomes an X for Unrated.

Query: If movies are literature, why aren't they unrated, like books? The point is they are rated and your movie will have to be, the way things are now. There are no scientific guidelines for you to follow to secure a specific rating. Your best judgment about just what sort of rating to expect on your movie shouldn't be considered the final word. I suggest you ask your distributor, who is knowledgeable about these matters, for his best guess. The ratings are all a matter of degree and as the times change, criteria for each rating will probably reflect changes in what the general adult public will accept as reasonable for children.

FOOD FOR THOUGHT

Since concession sales and resultant profits are so essential to exhibitors, they should prefer to play movies that arouse appetites for food. What kind of movies garner the highest patron response for food and drink? My own observations are that general audience movies, for children and parents together, account for the highest sales. These films would include movies made to entertain by putting a smile on people's faces and supply enough good-humored action to keep audiences active and alive, not serious and morose. For example, a movie dealing with automobile racing, a caper flick full of excitement and happy resolutions to crises, gets kids emotionally involved and ready for sugary candy and sweet tasting soda pop, especially if the popcorn is heavily salted.

Young people may have eaten lunch or dinner just a few hours before going to the movies. But, once there, aroused by action and empathic with the screen fantasy, their sweet-toothed appetites are activated. Older folk have gold fillings. They shy away from sticky candy for fear of losing a filling. They are mindful of caloric intake, weight problems, cholesterol, cavities, and dental bills. Kids are oblivious to these things. They just want to enjoy themselves and health isn't a worry, or even a thought. X-rated movies are terrible for concession sales, because X-rated audiences are older and so desirous of seeing what's on the screen that they lose their desire for eating. On the other hand, G-rated movies for patrons of any age cater to craving, hungering, thirsting, itching young audiences who lick their chops at the screen action and lust for junk food like a moth speeding to a flame. Movies dealing with action and violence bestir the blood and a rousing adventure gets the gastric juices flowing in young bellies. Mindless movies with boring exposition between action scenes are especially good for concession sales between interludes.

SPECIAL TREATMENT

Many people in the nation's dozen or so large cities don't go to see a movie unless they've read two or three reviews about the movie. I wonder if these readers realize that many critics are given special treatment. They're invited to premieres, flown around the country, wined and dined, given expense money, provided with special interviews with stars and with free publicity photos. Then they go home and write feature stories and reviews. How many of these bought and paid-for junketeer-critics are going to write unfavorable articles? Why do so many readers believe in the long articles in magazines and newspapers praising films not yet released? Some of the major film companies have such a stranglehold on the industry that they can, and would, do anything to insure that their movie will not lose money. These articles help to create a demand so that the film will get an immediate and lucrative television sale—a sale so big, that even if the public smells out the movie as a dog, the major will still have made money because a TV network bought the "dog" hook, line and sinker. In some cases, TV networks help bankroll theatrical movies, joining commercial production-distribution companies in "the selling of a movie—any movie."

A GREAT RESOURCE:
THE LIBRARY OF CONGRESS

Screenwriting students should consider spending a week in Washington, D.C. The Library of Congress has a print of nearly every movie made in the past thirty years. If you reserve the movies you want to see enough in advance, you can see and study film starting at 8:30 a.m. It is especially rewarding when you plan ahead and select a body of work that will have particular interest for you. There are also many scripts, on shelves PN 1995-7. You can take them to a desk and study all day. Can you beat it? You're doing what you like, it's free, and it's beneficial. Just as a physician, an accountant, architect or map-maker has his or her publications, a screenwriter has script. Just stop reading gossip columns about movies for a while. Forget them. Let the public buy the publicity about who said or did what to whom. Your task is not to pursue flackery and advertising handouts, but truths. Your object is not facts either, for facts are just selected truths, the kind that lawyers deal in. Truths are hard to find. You must have the will of a dedicated investigative reporter to quest for knowledge. Most people don't have that will, but if you want to be a professional screenwriter, you must. There is no alternative. Your equity is in your brain, not real estate.

INDUSTRY TRADE PUBLICATIONS

It is important, even essential, for aspiring film people to read industry trade publications such as the *Daily* or *Weekly Variety*, the *Daily Hollywood Reporter*, the weekly *Boxoffice Magazine* and weekly *Independent Film Journal*. These publications will acquaint you with the language of film, the idiomatic expressions used in hard news and feature articles about the commercial movie world. You'll be better prepared to talk the same language when you meet an experienced film person. Then you will begin to appreciate the time you took to learn some of the language of film.

"BRING 'EM BACK ALIVE"

What kind of movie should you be thinking of making? Note the kind of new releases hitting the market and *don't make them*. If there are lots of westerns in recent release, then I suggest you forget about them. On the other hand, if there are no westerns, then start scripting a western or two. All you'll need is a lucky break that a new western comes out and does big business. Hollywood is so cyclical, a land where the sheep follow the sheep, that readers and producers will then begin to search through their piles of shelved scripts for western stories. You may be one of the lucky ones who anticipated a trend simply because so many don't take advantage of the Hollywood mentality to "bring 'em back alive" as soon as the public demands a new genre of entertainment. Of course, year after year, the staples of horror and science-fiction movies remain your best bet, a hedge against all cycles. There is always a market for vehicle (racing cars, motorcycles, vans, trucks) action programmers.

TV: IT'S ACADEMIC

The tremendous demands by television for feature movies will undoubtedly continue. The emphasis will be on action flicks involving young people on the run, on the make, battling the establishment, competing with their peers, leading lives of danger and excitement. Many first-timers in the industry will again be turning to television for initial entry into the business. My advice is to watch all those first-run made-for-TV-movies situation comedies, and dramas; analyze them, time each shot, each scene, each sequence. Try to understand the rhythm; how often action occurs and how it takes place. Note how tension is built and conflict is dealt with. This requires time, concentration and note-taking. If you want to get into the business, you can't watch movies or TV for fun. You must watch film as an academic exercise if you want to profit from your experiences. There is just no way you can guess at making a movie.

WHY MANY REALTORS DON'T INVEST IN MOVIES

Let's suppose you approach real estate developers for $750,000 to produce your movie. They probably have the money or can get it through their line of credit or by using their property as collateral. What they are likely to tell you may come as a shock. With that kind of available hard cash, they can probably generate twenty to thirty million dollars worth of new housing, perhaps buy enough acreage, clear and develop it, build perhaps 250 single-family townhouses that might sell in the range of $60,000 to $120,000. And, even though the builder may be fully borrowed against his collateral, a bank is likely to provide 90 percent financing to the individual home buyers. Further, the way inflation is going, those homes might appreciate by a third in three or four years, perhaps going up in value from $60,000 to $80,000 or from $120,000 to $160,000, with a potential cash profit of from $20,000 to $40,000 to each homeowner! Or, if the homeowners get to that point and don't want to sell, they can increase their first mortgage or take out a second mortgage and get immediate cash on their asset. The home is collateral for the mortgage. It has real value in the marketplace. As for the builders, they are in good shape with tax shelters, tax write-offs, depreciation, profits and a good reputation as well.

On the other hand, what has the would-be film producer got to offer? Only a dream that may or may not come true. And what about potential profits and sheltering of taxes? Investors, like L'il Abner, do have their "druthers." Most times, they'd druther invest in real estate than movies. They get logical with you. They say real estate pays.

THE "WOMs"

In judging how a film will be received, you will always be dealing with the unknown. Guessing at audience reaction is a fool's game. WOM—word of mouth—is almost always what makes movies hits or duds. It's what people say, right from the start. Watch their facial expressions, their body language when they watch a movie or when they exit a theater lobby. Listen when they mumble in personal interaction. Note the people waiting in the lobby or line. They too will be looking at, watching and listening to the outgoing patrons, and are influenced by them at once. Later, audiences will talk about what movie they just saw, and again influence others. Audiences are opinion-makers, the carriers of good, bad, or indifferent tidings called "WOMs."

SPONSORED FILMS

There is another world in movies called "non-theatrical." It takes in all those films that aren't intended for exhibition to paying customers—that is, "sponsored films." There are about 15,000 to 25,000 sponsored films produced annually. The majority are made in the U.S.A. I would estimate that their combined budgets exceed $75 million. The goal of most U.S. productions is training or public information. These films range from pure education to propaganda. The U.S. government produces more than 80% of all sponsored films, and a majority of those are intended for foreign distribution. The films are meant to give information and persuade foreign audiences including people, industries and governments. The Fulbright Act prohibits domestic distribution of these films. There was one exception to this law: the film *John F. Kennedy: Years of Lightning, Day of Drums*. A special act of Congress permitted its exhibition in America. Supposedly, all profits were to go to the John F. Kennedy Center for the Performing Arts in Washington, D.C.; however, there was commercial distribution of this film.

Until recent times the monies expended for those films went directly into production. No allocation was made for distribution. Eventually, bureaucrats realized that no matter how good the movies were, they had to be seen to be appreciated. They had to be marketed, distributed, advertised and leased or sold. Like theatrical movies, sponsored films need an audience. Thus, funds were appropriated for distribution of these films. A film dormant on a shelf doesn't render profits. Profits were now to be measured in terms of how many people saw each movie. That's the way it is now. In 1968, the U.S. Government, realizing that confusion existed about the growing number of sponsored film programs, established a single cource for government films. The National Audiovisual Center of the National Archives was established as the central clearing house to coordinate distribution of films for public use. Income from sales and rentals are directed to the center to pay for operating expenses.

Now, with distribution coordinated, there still remained a need to coordinate film production, because more than one agency could plan to produce movies dealing with the same subject. To avoid duplication of goals and assignments, movie producers asked Congress to do something about the problem, and Congress, in turn, asked the executive branch to solve it. They did, in 1978, when the Office of Management and Budget (OMB) issued a government-wide policy to coordinate production. All government agencies are now required to check a central information file before they start production and report back to that central file when they finish their film. It's still a grand experiment, but OMB, Congress and the movie industry are satisfied with this progress in structuring film production starts.

All government agencies produce in-house films for their staffs and facilities. In addition, there are productions by contract, whereby agencies contract with producers to make films under the agencies' guidelines, subject to the agencies' final review. There is also production by grant, whereby nonprofit organizations deliver a finished film to an agency. Last, there is production of "outside" product. For example, a major automaker might produce a film for the National Highway Administration, for distribution. In this situation, the government agency would share all rights in the film with the automaker.

In the U.S., sponsored films made for domestic audiences are distributed about 70 percent of the time to educational institutions. The other 30 percent of the time, these nontheatrical films go to business and industry, or they are bought outright by libraries and other reference sources.

Most sponsored films are shot in 16mm, not 35mm. If a corporation wants to get a commercial message across, they blow up that 16mm negative into a 35mm print and exhibit it, mostly in small-town theaters as the theater's scheduling permits. Exhibitors don't mind showing them; they are usually boring, sending audiences to the concession stands to buy candy. These fillers are commercials advertising products and services to a captured audience. Theater audiences can't dial them out, like TV, but they can walk away from them.

Some young filmmakers earn a marginal living, doing one job or another on these films before they feel experienced enough to tackle feature movies.

GLOSSARY

Above the line: Generally, describes all budget items contracted for prior to production; almost always considered non-variable

Academy aperture: Screen ratio of 1:33 to 1, width to height; close to TV screen ratio

Alteration of contract terms: Review (reduction) of original film rental terms

B.G.: Background

Barn doors: Hinged, solid black doors used to control light during film production

Below the line: Generally, describes all budget items contracted for prior to, during and following production; variable costs

Best boy: First assistant to the gaffer; also, less commonly, the title for the key grip's first assistant

Box-office gross: Total monies received from ticket sales to public in a theater

Box-office statement: Exhibitor's report of box-office gross of movie in theater

Budget: Financial plan and cost

Camera angle:　View of set through camera

Camera dolly:　A wheeled platform capable of supporting the camera and camera operator; used for moving shots; often on railroad-like steel tracks

Camera grip:　A set grip assigned to camera department to assist in moving and setting up camera equipment

Chart town:　See **key city**

Coating:　Printing reference numbers on film and sound track as an aid in editing

Completion bond:　Guarantee of funds to insure completion of a movie

Continuity:　Arrangement of flow of events in a movie so they are logical, sequential, and matching

Crane:　Platform providing vertical movement for a camera

Cut:　To edit out; also, to command to stop filming; in a script, signifies an instantaneous change to another shot

Dailies:　Work print of a day's shooting. **Syn**: rushes

Director of photography:　Leading technical craftsperson of a movie; heads camera department, directs lighting and grip (other than camera) departments

Dissolve:　A gradual change out of one shot or scene to a gradual change into another shot or scene; usually indicates a passage of time

Dolly grip:　A technician assigned task of setting up and operating the camera dolly. See **grip**

Dolly shot:　A shot involving camera movement

Double:　Replacement for actor or actress during filming

Double bill:　Two movies on one program

Dubbing:　Re-recording of dialogue for better quality or into another language

Editing:　Assembling pieces of film into a coherent whole

85 filter:　A photographic device that converts daylight to 3200° Kelvin color temperature to assure true color on film

Exchange:　Major city in a geographic area in which a distributor maintains a sales office

Fade:　A gradual change into or out of a shot or scene from or to a blank visual; usually, fade-in at start of movie and fade-out at end; a transition device

Film booker: Exhibitor who arranges for a playdate on a film in a theater

Film buyer: Exhibitor who contracts for film to play in theater

Film rental: Distributor's charge to exhibitor for leasing a movie

Fine cut: Assembly of movie in final stages of editing

Floor: Minimum distribution film rental terms to exhibitor

Floor plans: Diagram of layout of a movie set

Frame: One image on photographic film; also, composition

Franchise holder: Independent distributor

Gaffer: Chief electrician and lighting technician on a movie set

General commercial releases: Movies that play the mainstream of American theaters

Grip: A technician assigned to handling most equipment and handling grip equipment; i.e.: camera, furniture

Hooks: Connective links from shot to shot and scene to scene

House nut: Weekly house expense; cost of running a theater weekly as agreed to by distributor and exhibitor

Hyphenated-person: Individual receiving credit for more than one activity; i.e.: producer-director

Internegative: Intermediary negative made to protect the original negative; positive prints are made from the internegative

Key city: Usually the bigger grossing cities in each exchange areas **Syn:** chart town

Key grip: Chief set technician responsible for handling most equipment and operating all grip equipment

Location: A place where films are made in real-life environments

Looping: Re-recording dialogue during post-production for better quality, or for addition to sound track.

Major company: Generally, a member of the Motion Picture Association of America (M.P.A.A.)

Mix: Combining all sound elements with visuals; final stage of post-production

Movie ratings: Suggested guidelines for audiences established by M.P.A.A.

Negative: See **raw stock**

Nets: Cloth mesh for screening light

Non-theatrical: Describes a film not intended for a paying audience in a theater

Nuance: Any characteristic repeated during a movie

O.S.: Off-scene

Offshore: Overseas; a U.S. distribution term

On the one hand-on the other hand: A script concept to stimulate ideas and create drama through opposites

1.85 to 1: Screen ratio in which most movies are photographed, width to height

Opticals: Visual effects added to a film during postproduction

Parallels: Scaffolding

Playdate: The dates film will be shown in a theater

Polish: A refinement of a script

Postproduction: Completion work on a movie; includes editing, scoring, mixing, opticals, titles

POV: Point of view

Preproduction: Preparation work on a movie; includes financing, planning, testing and contracting for labor, materials, locations

Principal photography: Actual filming of a movie. **Syn:** shoot.

Proposal: A complete disclosure of all truths relevant to intended production

Raw stock: Unexposed film used to photograph movie; the negative

Release print: A final print of the film sent to theater for exhibition

Rigging: Rope, pipe, lumber, and so forth.

Rushes: See **dailies**

Scenario: Story line for a movie

Scene: A collection of shots and/or a setting

Scoring: Music for a movie

Scratch sound: Recorded sync sound while filming; insufficient for use, but used as an aid for later dubbing

Screenplay: See **script**

Scrims: Metal mesh that fits in front of light; controls intensity of light

Script: Master plan for a movie

Script breakdown: An analysis of a script by separating it into its component parts

Sequence: Usually a continuous period of time; contains several scenes

Set: The place where filming is done, or the actual place being filmed

Setup: Every time the camera and/or lighting is changed on a shoot

Shoot: See **principal photography**

Shot: Action contained on a single continuous length of film

Shot list: A list of shots to be photographed

Silks: White cloths for modifying light

Sliding scale: A method of determining film rental based on theater overhead

Soft lights: Indirect lighting

Special effects: Anything that can't be filmed naturally

Sponsored film: A nontheatrical film financed by an interested party to promote special interests

Spots: Commercial announcements

Stand-in: A replacement for actor or actress during rehearsals

Studio: A place where films are made

Sync sound: Sound recorded to precisely match the visual

Take: A single passage of film through the camera

Theater circuit: A single exhibition company, owning and operating more than one theater

Timing: The determination of correct color balance of a work print; a laboratory function.

Titles: Credits for people and company who made the movie and title of movie

Trailers: Coming attraction spots in movie theaters

Treatment: Complete expression of film idea in prose form

V.O.: Voice Over

Wipe: A change of scene, usually accomplished by a vertical line moving horizontally across the frame; a transition device

WOM: Word of mouth

Wrap: Expression signifying the end of film work

Zoom Lens: Variable focal length lens

INDEX

Above-the-line expenses,
  summary of, 63
Action, 24, 35
Actors:
  auditioning, 99–100
  fees of leads, 61
  fees of supporting, 62
Adjectives, use of, 20
Adverbs, use of, 20
Advertising costs, 137
Advisors, 74–75
Agency form, 183
Art directors, fee, 79–80
Assistant director:
  fees, 71
  script breakdown, 113–121

Below-the-line costs, 64–69
Box-office receipts, 144–145

Box-office statements:
  charting, 163–167
  grosses, 153–154
Budgeting movies. See Costs

Casting director, 74
Color, 35
Conflict, 34
Continuity script staff, 70–71
Contract terms, exhibitors',
  156
Costs, above-the-line:
  director, 59
  extras, 62
  lead actors, 61
  producer and assistant, 59
  production staff, 64–81
  story and screenplay, 58
  supporting actors, 62

Costs, distribution. See
    Distribution
Costs, post-production:
    editing, 82
    insurance, 87
    legal, 87
    locations, 85–86
    music, 84
    studios, 85–86
    tests, 86
Costs, production. See
    Production staff
Critics, 181

Define, describe, compare,
    contrast, 18–19
Dialogue, 36
Director:
    fees, 59
    script samples, 125
Distribution:
    advertising costs, 137
    exhibitor relations,
        148–153
    film rental terms, 154
    key cities, 131–135
    majors, minors,
        independents, 136–137
    overseas, 147–148
    by producer, 148–153
    terms for exhibitors,
        170–176
    See also Exhibitors
Distributors, independent,
    135–137

Editing, costs, 82–84
Electrical department, costs,
    77–78

Exercises for screenwriters,
    30–31, 51–52
Exhibition:
    costs, 165
    house nuts, 167–168
    multiple screens, 165–166
    rental terms, 171–174
Exhibition contract, 153
Expenses. See Costs
Extras, fee, 62

Fally Marcus, 179
Fees, screenwriters', 33–36. See
    also Costs
Film:
    production costs, 81–82
    rental terms, 154–156,
        171–176
Financial arrangements, 94
Full disclosure, 91

Glossary, 195–199
Good-guy, bad-guy, 33
Grips, fees, 78
Grosses. See Box-office
    statements
Gross film rentals, 138–144

Hooks, 27–28
House nuts, 167–168

Independent moviemakers,
    55–56
Inner ear, inner eye, 14–15
Insurance costs, 87
Introductory premise, 10–13
Introductory treatment, 12–
    14
Investments in movies, 190

Key cities, 131–135

Laboratory fees, 82
Leasing movies, 166–167
Legal:
    consequences, 95–96
    costs, 88
Library of Congress, 188
Location forms, 69
Locations, costs of on-site, 86

Major distributors, 135–137
Makeup:
    fees, 80
    planning checklist, 102
Middleman. See Distributor
Movie buffs, 181
Multiple screens, 165–166
Music, costs, 84

Nuances and hooks, 24–29

Offshore distribution. See
    Overseas Distribution
Overseas distribution, 147–
    148

Personal pronouns, in
    screenwriting, 34
Photography, director, 74–75
PM. See Production manager
Premise:
    expanding, 12
    introductory, 10
Preproduction costs. See Costs
Producer, associate, fee for,
    59
Producer fees, 59
Production assistants, 71–74

Production manager:
    location form, 69
    tasks, 64–69
Production process:
    auditioning actors, 99
    dressing actors, 100
    dressing sets, 103
    sample script, 104–112
    schedules, 121–122
    shot list, 118–122
    special effects, 104
Production report, 67
Production staff:
    advisors, 74
    art director, 79
    assistants, 71–72
    clerks, 73
    continuity, script, 70–71
    electrical, 77
    grips, 78
    list of, 66
    manager, 64–69
    photography director,
        75–76
    sources of, 78
Property, personnel, 80
Proposal:
    financial arrangements, 94
    full disclosure, 91
    industry history, 92
    legal consequences, 95
    resumés of staff, 94
    script synopsis, 93
    tax consequences, 96
Publicity costs, 86

Ratings, MPAA system, 186
Release forms, 69
Rental terms. See Film rentals

Retailing movies, 161–169
Rewriting, 40

Screenplay costs, 58. *See also*
  Screenwriting
Screens, exhibitors, types,
  162
Screenwriting:
  define, describe,
    compare, contrast,
    18–19
  fees, 43–46
  good guys, bad guys, 33
  introductory premise, 10
  nuances and hooks, 24–29
  on-the-one-hand, on-
    the-other-hand, 12
  premise, 11
  script, 6–32
  speaking it, 9
  supposes, 29–32
  treatment, complete,
    15–20
  treatment, introductory,
    12
Script:
  breakdown of, 122–126
  detailed example, 104–
    112
  floor plans, 116–119
  synopsis of, for proposal,
    93
Scriptwriting. See Screenwriting

Sets:
  dressing, 103
  list of, 100
Short takes, 179–193
Shot list, 118–122
Sliding scales, for film rentals,
  172–176
Sound:
  personnel costs, 78–79
  post-production costs, 84
Special effects:
  fees for, 80
  preplanning, 104
Sponsored films, 191–192
Story board, 122
Story, costs, 58
Studios, costs, 85–86
Supporting actors. See Actors
Supposes, 29–32

Taxes:
  as cost, 87
  in proposal, 96
Tests of equipment, 86
Theater circuits, 162–163
Training programs, 185–186
Treatment:
  complete, 15–20
  introductory, 12
Trends, moviemaking, 50–51

Wardrobe:
  costs, 80
  planning, 100–102

Sheldon Tromberg has spent many years in the movie industry as producer, distributor, screenwriter, exhibitor, consultant, critic, and educator. As associate professor at the renowned Corcoran School of Art, he teaches film; and for many years taught filmmaking at Georgetown University. He is Executive Director, National Center for Advanced Film Studies and Services; President of TNT Productions; a director of the Motion Picture Advisors of America; and a talk show host on WRC Radio, NBC's Washington, D.C. affiliate.

His movies, *Teenage Graffiti* and *The Redeemers* have been distributed worldwide by Allied Artists and Dimension Pictures, respectively. He previously produced the Children's Film Festival. Tromberg has himself distributed more than 2,000 feature films, traveling throughout the country to most of the sites mentioned in this book, including cities, towns, and institutions. He has written a number of screenplays, including *The Silver Dollar Caper, The Strange Case of April Springer, To Live Forever, Junkyard USA,* and *Rock 'n Roll America.*

Professor Tromberg is a frequent contributor to the "Op Ed" column of the *Baltimore Sun* and has also written for the *Los Angeles Times, Washington Post, Washingtonian Magazine, Men's Digest,* and *Turf and Sport Digest.*

Professor Tromberg, a graduate of Columbia University, has a master's degree in Public Administration and a doctorate in Business Administration. A long-time resident of Washington, D.C., he is married and has three children.